PRAISE FOR
The Saint, the Surfer, and the CEO

"If you are ready to live your best life now, read this extraordinary book." Richard Carlson, Ph.D., author of the #1 *New York Times* bestseller *Don't Sweat the Small Stuff*

"Another amazing, life-changing book by Robin Sharma." Mark Victor Hansen, co-creator of the #1 *New York Times* bestselling series *Chicken Soup for the Soul*®; co-author of *The One Minute Millionaire*

"This book will touch—and change—many lives." John Gray, author of the international bestseller *Men Are from Mars, Women Are from Venus*

PRAISE FOR
The Monk Who Sold His Ferrari

"Nothing less than sensational. This book will bless your life." Mark Victor Hansen

"A captivating story that teaches as it delights." Paulo Coelho, author of *The Alchemist*

"This is a fun, fascinating, fanciful adventure into the realms of personal development, personal effectiveness and individual happiness. It contains treasures of wisdom that can enrich and enhance the life of every single person." Brian Tracy, author of *Maximum Achievement*

"Robin S. Sharma has an important message for all of us — one that can change our lives. He's written a one-of-a-kind handbook for personal fulfillment in a hectic age." Scott DeGarmo, past publisher, *Success Magazine*

"Robin Sharma has created an enchanting tale that incorporates the classic tools of transformation into a simple philosophy of living. A delightful book that will change your life." Elaine St. James, author of *Simplify Your Life* and *Inner Simplicity*

D0375523

Also by Robin Sharma

The Saint, the Surfer, and the CEO
The Monk Who Sold His Ferrari
Family Wisdom from The Monk Who Sold His Ferrari
MegaLiving

For more information on Robin Sharma's books,
audio programs, videos, and learning tools, please visit:
www.robinsharma.com and **www.hayhouse.com**

Leadership Wisdom from The Monk Who Sold His Ferrari

Published and distributed in the United States by: Hay House, Inc., P.O. Box 5100, Carlsbad, CA 92018-5100 • (800) 654-5126 • (800) 650-5115 (fax) • www.hayhouse.com • **Published and distributed in Australia by:** Hay House Australia Pty Ltd, P.O. Box 515, Brighton-Le-Sands, NSW 2216 • *phone:* 1800 023 516 • *e-mail:* info@hayhouse.com.au • **Distributed in the United Kingdom by:** Airlift, 8 The Arena, Mollison Ave., Enfield, Middlesex, United Kingdom EN3 7NL

Text design: Karen Petherick

Originally published by Harper Collins Publishers Ltd, Toronto, Canada. Copyright © 1998 • ISBN: 0-00-638562-1

Library of Congress Cataloging-in-Publication Data

Sharma, Robin.
  Leadership wisdom from the monk who sold his Ferrari : the 8 rituals of visionary leaders / 5 Robin Sharma.
      p. cm.
    ISBN 1-40190-013-5 (tradepaper)
    1. Leadership. I. Title.
    HD57.7 .S476 2003
    338.4'7005'0684—dc21

                                                    2002007670

                              ISBN 1-4019-0013-5

                     06   05   04   03   4 3 2 1
                   1st Hay House printing, January 2003

                              Printed in Canada

Leadership Wisdom from The Monk Who Sold His Ferrari

The 8 Rituals of Visionary Leaders

Robin Sharma

A Fable

Hay House, Inc.
Carlsbad, California • Sydney, Australia
Canada • Hong Kong • United Kingdom

To my daughter, Bianca. May you always be
the model of joy.

To the many readers of *The Monk Who Sold His Ferrari*
who took the time out of their busy lives to tell
me how this simple book touched them.
You have moved me.

And to all those leaders who deeply honor the
sacred trust between them and the people they have the
privilege to lead. Keep blessing lives and liberating talent.

❦

*This is the true joy in life, being used for a purpose recognized by
yourself as a mighty one, being a true force of Nature instead of a
feverish little clod of ailments and grievances complaining that the
world will not devote itself to making you happy. . . . I want to be
thoroughly used up when I die. For the harder I work, the more I live.
I rejoice in life for its own sake. Life is no brief candle to me. It's a sort
of splendid torch which I've got to hold up for the moment and I want
to make it burn as brightly as possible before handing it on to future
generations.*

George Bernard Shaw

CONTENTS

ACKNOWLEDGMENTS

I express deep appreciation to my extraordinary team at Sharma Leadership International for your wonderful support. Thanks also go to our corporate clients for offering me the privilege of speaking at your conferences and working to create leaders at all levels of the organization. Special thanks must go, as well, to all of the readers of *The Monk Who Sold His Ferrari*, *Who Will Cry When You Die?* and *The Saint, the Surfer, and the CEO*, who so kindly shared my message with those who needed to hear it. I also express deep appreciation to Jill Kramer, Danny Levin, and Reid Tracy and the entire team at Hay House for believing in me.

To my colleagues Richard Carlson, Mark Victor Hansen, John Gray, Wayne Dyer, and Nido Qubein, I am grateful for your encouragement.

Finally, I thank my parents for your endless support; my brother, Sanjay, and my sister-in-law, Susan, for your kindness (and Neel); and my two extraordinary children, Colby and Bianca, for all your love.

CHAPTER ONE

A Wild Ride to Success

IT WAS THE SADDEST DAY of my life. As I arrived at work after a rare long weekend spent hiking and laughing in the mountains with my kids, I saw two enormous security guards hunched over the mahogany desk in my coveted corner office. Running closer, I could see that they were rifling through my files and peeking into the precious documents on my laptop computer, oblivious to the fact that I had spotted them. Finally, one of them noticed me standing there, my face flushed with anger, my hands shaking at the sight of this unforgivable invasion. With an expression that revealed not a hint of emotion, he looked at me and spoke fifteen words that left me feeling as if I'd just been kicked in the chest: "Mr. Franklin, you have been fired. We must escort you out of the building immediately."

With that simple dispatch, I went from being the senior vice president of the fastest-growing software company on the continent to a man without a future. And believe me, I took my dismissal very hard. Failure was a foreign concept to me, an experience I had no idea how to manage. In college, I'd been a golden boy, the kid with the perfect grades, the beautiful girls, and the boundless future. I made the varsity track team, was elected class president, and even found the time to host a hugely popular jazz show on our campus radio station. It seemed to all concerned that I was gifted and destined for great success. One day I overheard one of my old professors saying to a colleague, "If I had the chance to live my life over again, I'd like to come back as Peter Franklin."

Mind you, my talents were not as natural as everyone believed. The true source of my achievements could be traced back to a punishing work ethic and an almost obsessive desire to win. My father had come to this country as a penniless immigrant many years ago with a deeply held vision of a more tranquil, prosperous, and happy life for his young family. He changed our family name, settled us into a three-room apartment in a good part of town, and started working tirelessly as a factory worker for minimum wage, a job he would keep for the next forty years of his life. And although he had no formal education, I'd never met a wiser man — until recently, when I met a most extraordinary human being, a person whom you truly must get to know. I promise to tell you more about him shortly. You will never be the same.

My father's dream for me was a simple one: get a first-class education at a first-class school. A career of peak achievement and just compensation would then be assured, or so he thought. His firm belief was that a well-developed base of personal knowledge laid the foundation for a successful life. "No matter what happens to you, Peter, no one will ever be able to take away your education. Knowledge will always be your best friend, no matter where you go or what you do," he would often say to me while finishing his supper after another grueling fourteen-hour day at the factory he devoted most of his life to. My father was quite a man.

He was also a great storyteller, one of the best. In his home country, the elders used parables to convey the wisdom of the ages to their children, so he carried this rich tradition with him to his adopted country. From the day that my mother died suddenly while making his lunch in our well-worn kitchen until the time that my brother and I entered our teenage years, my father would send us off to a dreamy sleep with a delightful story that always had a life lesson. One that particularly stands out in my mind is about an old farmer on his deathbed, who asked his three sons to gather around him. "Sons," he said, "Death is close by and I shall soon take my last breath. But before I do, I must share a secret with you. In that field behind our farmhouse, there lies a glorious treasure. Dig deep and you shall find it. You will never have to worry about money again."

Once the old man had died, the sons ran out to the field and started digging with wild abandon. They dug for many hours and continued for many days. No part of the field was left untilled as they put every ounce of their youthful energy into this task. But, alas, no treasure could be found. Eventually, they gave up, cursing their father for his apparent deception and wondering why he would choose to make such fools of them. However, the following fall, that same field yielded a harvest the likes of which the entire community had never seen before. The three sons quickly became rich. And they never worried about money again.

So, from my father, I learned the power of dedication, diligence, and hard work. In my college days, I toiled day and night, eager to stay on the dean's list and to fulfill the dreams my dad had set for me. I won scholarship after scholarship and diligently sent my aging father a small check at the end of every month, a portion of the salary I received from the part-time job that I held.

This was a simple token of thanks for all he had done. When it came time to enter the work force, I had already been offered a lucrative management position in the high-tech field, the field of my choice. The company was called Digitech Software Strategies, and it was the place where everyone wanted to work.

Astonishingly successful, the pundits predicted that its meteoric growth would only continue, and I felt truly honored that the firm had actively recruited me to become a member of its high-flying team. Quickly accepting the post, I began working eighty-hour weeks to prove that I was worth every penny of the lofty salary I received. Little did I know that, seven years later, the very same company would humiliate me as I had never been humiliated before.

The first few years at Digitech were good ones. They really were. I made some fine friends, learned a great deal, and quickly rose through the executive ranks. I became the acknowledged superstar, a young man who had a razor-sharp mind, who knew how to work hard and who showed true commitment to the company. Although I'd never really been taught how to manage and lead people, they just kept on promoting me to ever-higher positions of responsibility.

But, without a doubt, the best thing that happened to me at Digitech Software Strategies was meeting Samantha, the woman who would eventually become my wife. A bright young manager herself, she was strikingly pretty, with a formidable intellect to match. After meeting at the Christmas party, we quickly hit it off and were soon spending what little free time we had together. From day one, Samantha was my greatest fan, a true believer in my potential and talent. "Peter, you'll be the CEO," she would regularly tell me, giving me a soft smile. "I know you've got what it takes." Unfortunately, not everyone felt the same way. Or perhaps they did.

The CEO of Digitech Software ruled the company like a dictator. A self-made man with a vicious streak, he had an ego that matched his grossly inflated paycheck. When I first started working with him, he was polite though reserved. But when word started to spread about my abilities and my ambitions, he grew cold, often communicating with me through terse memos when the situation called for something less formal. Samantha called him an "insecure little clod of a man," but the fact remained that he had power. Real power. Maybe he felt that as I rose to higher management positions, I would make him look bad. Or maybe he saw too much of himself in me — and didn't like what he saw.

I have to admit, however, that I carried my own weaknesses. Foremost was a hair-trigger temper. If something went wrong at the wrong time, a rage brewed within me that I simply could not control. I have no idea where it came from, but it was there. And it was not a business asset. I'll also admit that although I think I'm a fundamentally decent person, I could be a little rough around the edges when it came to the art of managing people. Like I said, I had never received any leadership training and operated on what little instinct I had been granted. I often felt that not everyone on my team shared my work ethic and commitment to excellence, which led me to frustration. Yes, I would yell at people. Yes, I took on far more responsibility than I was capable of handling. Yes, I should have spent more time building relationships and cultivating loyalty. But there were always too many fires to put out, and I never seemed to have enough time to attend to the things that needed improving. I guess I was like the mariner who spent all his time bailing water out of his boat rather than taking the time to fix the hole in it. Shortsighted at best.

And so the day came when I was fired. The months that followed were truly the darkest of my life. Thank God I had Samantha and the kids around me. They did their best to lift my spirits and encourage me to pick up the pieces of my once fast-track career. But those months of idleness showed me that our self-esteem is linked to our jobs. At a cocktail party, the first question we are inevitably asked is: "So what do you do for a living?" As we began our weekly round of golf, my partners would always ask, "Any news on work, Peter?" The doorman at our luxury high-rise, always a master of small talk, would regularly inquire whether things were going well at the office. With no job to go to, I no longer had any answers.

I went from getting up in the morning and rushing off to the subway station, my mind full of ideas, to awakening around noon in a darkened room, littered with empty Heineken bottles, Marlboro packages, and sticky Häagen-Dazs containers. I stopped reading the *Wall Street Journal* and retreated into cheesy spy novels, old Western paperbacks, and trashy tabloids that revealed that Oprah was an alien and that Elvis was still alive, managing a McDonald's on the West Coast. I could not face reality. I just didn't want to think too hard or do too much. A numbing pain pervaded my body, and resting under the covers of our four-poster bed seemed like the best place to be.

Then one day, I received a phone call. It was an old college friend who had carved out an excellent reputation as one of the best minds in the software industry. He told me that he had just quit his job as chief programmer for a large company and was getting ready to start his own firm. I still recall him telling me that he had what he called "a brilliant concept" for a new line of software and needed a partner he could trust. I was his first choice. "It's a chance to build something great, Peter," he said with his usual sense of enthusiasm. "C'mon. It'll be fun."

Part of me lacked the confidence to say yes. Starting a new business is never easy, especially in the high-tech field. What if we failed? As it was, our financial situation was a mess. As senior vice president at Digitech Software, I was paid well and lived the kind of life that my father could only have dreamed of. I drove a brand-new BMW while Samantha had her own Mercedes. The kids went to private school and spent summers at a prestigious sailing camp. My golf club's membership fees alone totaled the annual income of many of my friends. Now, with no job, the unpaid bills were piling up and many promises were being broken. It was not the ideal time to dream of my own business.

On the other hand, my wise father always told me that "nothing can defeat you unless you defeat yourself." I needed this opportunity to lift me from the darkness that had enveloped my life. I needed a reason to wake up in the morning. I needed to reconnect to that sense of passion and purpose I had felt in college when I believed that I was unstoppable and the world was truly a place of unlimited possibilities. I had enough intuition to know that life sends us gifts from time to time. Success comes to those who recognize and accept them. So I said yes.

We grandly named the company GlobalView Software Solutions and set up shop in a tiny office in a run-down industrial complex. I was CEO and my partner was the self-appointed chairman. We had no employees, no furniture, and no money. But we did have a great idea. And so we started pitching our software concept to the marketplace. Fortunately, the marketplace enthusiastically responded. Soon Samantha came to work with us and we hired other employees. Our innovative software products began to sell at a phenomenal pace, and our profits quickly soared. That first year of operation, *Business Success* magazine listed us as one of the country's fastest-growing companies. My father was so proud. Though he was eighty-six at the time, I still remember him carrying a huge basket of fruit into the office to celebrate our achievement. Tears streamed down his face when he looked at me and said, "Son, your mother would have been very happy today."

That was more than eleven years ago, and we have continued our blistering pace of growth. GlobalView Software Solutions is now a two-billion-dollar company with 2,500 employees at eight locations around the world. Just last year we moved into our new international headquarters, a world-class complex complete with a state-of-the-art manufacturing facility, three Olympic-sized swimming pools, and an amphitheater for meetings and other corporate events. My partner is no longer involved in the day-to-day operations of the company and spends most of his time on his private island in the Caribbean or mountain-climbing in Nepal. Samantha left the leadership of the company a few years ago to pursue her passion for writing and to become more involved in community service. As for me, I'm still the CEO, but now I have crushing responsibilities that consume the majority of my time. Twenty-five hundred people look to me for their livelihoods, and many thousands more depend on our organization to provide products and services that help them in their daily lives.

Sadly, my father died two years after the company was formed, and though he always sensed I would be enormously successful, I don't think that even he could have imagined that we would be where we are today. I do miss, him but with all that's on my plate, I have little time to reflect on the past. I still work hard, about eighty hours in a good week. I haven't taken a real vacation in years and I'm as hard-driving, ambitious and competitive as I was the day I started work as a twenty-three-year-old kid at Digitech Software Strategies. Until I had the good fortune to meet a very special teacher a relatively short while ago, I still tried to do too much and micromanage every aspect of the business. I knew this was a weakness, but I seemed to have succeeded in spite of it.

Until that most memorable meeting, which I am about tell you about in greater detail, I still had my bad temper, a characteristic that had only worsened as the pressures on me had grown along with my business. And, despite the passage of time, I still had a hard time managing and motivating people. Oh, sure, my employees listened to me. But it was not because they wanted to — it's because they had to. They had no loyalty to me and no real commitment to the company. Fear rather than respect seemed to be the reason they would carry out the commands I issued from my palatial executive suite. It seemed that all my power stemmed solely from my position. And I knew that was a bad position to be in.

Let me share a little more with you about the challenges I faced as the leader of a fast-growing company in these turbulent and change-crazed times. Despite the expansion of our business, morale had plummeted. I had heard through the grapevine that some people were saying we had grown too quickly and that profits had become more important than people. Others complained that they were being forced to work too hard with not enough resources to support them. Still others complained that the tremendous change they faced on a daily basis, ranging from innovations in technology to new structures within the bureaucracy, left their heads spinning and their bodies tingling with stress. There was little trust, low productivity, and even less creativity. And from what I could gather, nearly everyone in the organization believed that the blame for the problems rested squarely with one person: me. The consensus was that I just did not know how to lead.

Although GlobalView Software continued to grow, the indicators started to show that we might be headed for our first loss in many years. Although our programs still continued to sell, we were losing market share. Our people were simply not as innovative and inspired as in the early days. As a result, our products were not as well designed and unique. To put it simply: people just didn't seem to care anymore. And I knew that if allowed to continue, that mindset would eventually spell the end of our company.

Signs of apathy were everywhere. Offices were disorganized and people were consistently late. Christmas parties were poorly attended and teamwork was almost nonexistent. Conflict was routine and initiative poor. Even our new manufacturing facility began to show signs of disrepair and neglect, its once gleaming floors now littered with trash and grime.

Remarkably, all that has changed. GlobalView Software Solutions is a truly excellent company again. And I know we are growing to be even better. Our organization has been transformed through the application of a very special leadership formula given to me by a very special man. This simple yet extraordinarily powerful system has brought back the excitement that once pervaded the entire company, inspired our people to new heights of commitment, sent productivity soaring, and caused our profits to skyrocket beyond even my wildest dreams. Our employees have become deeply loyal and dedicated to our shared vision for the future. They work as a dynamic and highly competent team. Even better, they love coming to work, and I love working with them. We all know we have discovered something magical, and we know we are now headed for something very big. Just last week, *Business Success* magazine featured me on the cover. The heading read simply, "The GlobalView Miracle: How One Company Grew Great."

So what is this miraculous and time-honored leadership formula that has made me the toast of the business community? Who was this wise visitor who revolutionized our organization and showed me how to become the kind of visionary leader these topsy-turvy times call for? I know with all my heart that the answers to these questions will change the way you lead as well as the way you live. The time has come for you to discover them.

CHAPTER TWO

A Monk in My Rose Garden

IT WAS A BIZARRE SCENE. Now that I reflect on it, I still cannot believe it happened. I had just come out of my regular Monday morning meeting with my managers after hearing that GlobalView's fortunes were going from bad to worse. In the meeting, one manager had informed me that some of our top programmers were thinking of going to work for a smaller company where their efforts would be more appreciated. He also said that the relationships between management and nonmanagement were growing more strained by the day. "They don't trust us anymore," he said angrily.

Another manager added, "Not only that, there's no teamwork in this place. Before we got so big, everyone would help one another. People truly cared about a job well done. In the old days, if we were under a deadline to ship out a big order, I still remember that all of us would work together, sometimes late into the night. I even remember times when the programmers and managers rolled up their sleeves to help people in shipping seal boxes and get them ready for loading onto the delivery trucks. Now it's every person for himself. It's a bunker mentality. I really can't stand it anymore."

Although I remained uncharacteristically calm during the meeting, I broke into a sweat as I walked down the long hallway that linked the boardroom to my office. The tension of the past few months was killing me, and I knew I had to do something to stop the company's downward spiral. I just didn't know who to talk to or what to do. Sure, I could hire a team of consultants to offer some quick-fix solutions to the problems that plagued us. But I felt I had to dig deeper to strike at the roots of what had caused us to go from being a visionary company full of passionate and compassionate people to a bulky bureaucracy where people could not wait for closing time.

By the time I reached my office, perspiration dripped off my forehead and my shirt was soaked. My executive assistant, seeing my state, rushed toward me and grabbed my arm. As she escorted me to the plush leather couch that sat next to one of the many floor-to-ceiling bookcases in my imperial office, she asked if she should call my doctor or perhaps even an ambulance. Not even giving her the courtesy of a reply, I lay down on the couch and closed my eyes. I had read somewhere that visualizing a soothing scene in the mind's eye was a great way to calm down after a stressful encounter. And so I did my best.

Just as I began to relax, I was startled by a loud noise. It sounded as if someone had thrown a rock against one of the windows in my office. I leapt to my feet and ran to the large main window in search of the culprit. But I could see no one. Maybe the stress I had been suffering from was playing games with my imagination. As I slowly returned to the couch, it happened again, but this time even louder. *Who could it be?* I wondered, thinking I should have my assistant call security immediately. *Probably another disgruntled computer programmer pushing his luck with the boss,* I thought, growing even more annoyed at the disturbance. I darted to the window yet another time and, this time, saw a figure standing in the center of the sweeping rose garden that my second-floor office overlooked. As I squinted my eyes and looked more carefully, I was shocked by what I saw.

It was a striking young man who appeared to be wearing a hooded red robe, the kind I'd seen the Tibetan monks wear on a trip that I had made to that exotic land more than a decade earlier. As the rays of the sun illuminated the handsome, unlined face of the stranger, his robe flapped in the light wind, giving him a mysterious, almost ethereal appearance. He had a big smile on his face. And on his feet he wore sandals.

After realizing that this was not some hallucination of an overworked CEO whose company was slowly sliding into oblivion, I pounded on the window in anger. The young man did not move. He remained in a fixed position and kept smiling. Then he offered me an enthusiastic wave. I could not stand this kind of disrespect. This clown was trespassing on my property, spoiling my rose garden and clearly attempting to make a fool out of me. I immediately commanded my executive assistant, Arielle, to call security. "Have them bring our strange visitor up to my office right now, before he gets away," I ordered. "He needs to be taught a lesson — the likes of which he will never forget."

Within minutes, four security guards were at my door, one of them carefully holding the young stranger, who appeared to be cooperating with them, by the arm. Surprisingly, the young man was still smiling, and he radiated a sense of strength and serenity as he stood in the doorway to my office. He did not appear to be a bit concerned about being caught by security and marched into my office. And although he said nothing, I was also struck by the strange feeling that I was in the presence of a man of great knowledge. I experienced the same feeling I used to have when I was with my dad. I really cannot explain it any more than that. Call it intuition, but my gut told me that the young man was far wiser than his youthful face showed. Actually, I think it was his eyes that gave it away.

In my years in business, I have discovered that a person's eyes can reveal the truth. They can disclose warmth, insecurity, insincerity, or integrity, if one simply takes the time to study them. The young man's eyes told me he had wisdom. They also indicated he had a passion for life and perhaps a slight mischievous streak. They seemed to sparkle when the sunlight pouring into my office caught them. Seen up close, the young man's ruby-red robe was quite splendid in its texture and design. And despite being inside, he had chosen to leave the hood on, lending further mystery to his remarkable appearance.

"Who are you and why were you throwing rocks at my window?" I demanded, my face growing hot and my palms growing even more sweaty.

The young man remained silent, his full lips holding their smile. Then he started to move his hands, bringing them together in a prayer stance, offering me the traditional greeting of the people of India.

This guy is unbelievable! I thought. *First he treads through my rose garden, the garden I love looking at from my office when things get crazy. Then he starts pitching rocks at my window, scaring the heck out of me. And now, when he is surrounded by four burly, no-nonsense security guards who could floor him in an instant, he plays games with me.*

"Look, kid, I don't know who you are or where you've come

from, and to be honest, I don't really care," I exclaimed. "You can keep wearing that silly robe and giving me that silly smile. Be as cocky as you like, because I plan to call the police. But before I do, why don't you break that vow of silence you monks are so famous for and tell me why you are here?"

"I'm here to help you reinvent your leadership, Peter," the young man replied in a surprisingly commanding tone. "I'm here to help you get your organization back on track. And then on to world-class status."

How did he know my name? Maybe this guy was dangerous. *I'm glad I've got security right in front of me,* I thought to myself. And what was all this nonsense about helping me reinvent my leadership and get my company back on track? If this clown was some kind of consultant trying to get my attention for a fat contract, he was going about it the wrong way. Why didn't he just send me a proposal like the rest of those overpriced, underworked consultants who have an amazing gift for creating busywork projects that ensure they never miss the target dates for their early retirements.

"You have no idea who I am, do you, Peter?" he asked in a friendly tone.

"No, I'm sorry I don't. And if you don't tell me now, I'm going to kick your sorry behind down the hallway and out into the parking lot!" I yelled menacingly.

"I see you still have that temper, Peter. We'll need to work on that. I'll bet it doesn't help you win the loyalty of your team. And I know it does nothing but hurt your golf game, which never was that good," said the young man, breaking into a laugh.

"Do you have any idea who you are talking to, you arrogant little troublemaker?" I screamed, disregarding the fact that the mysterious stranger was well over six feet tall and in superb physical condition. "How dare you chastise me for my temper? And how do you know so much about my golf game? If you've been following me around, I'm definitely getting the police to charge you. That's a very serious offense, you know," I noted, whipping myself into a frenzy that caused me to sweat profusely once again.

Then the young man did something that astonished me. He lifted his hand and reached deep into his robe, pulling out what appeared to be a gold-plated golf ball. He then tossed it high into the air for me to catch. "I thought you might want it back," he remarked, still smiling.

I was stunned by the object now resting in the palm of my hand. For the golf ball carried an inscription: *To Julian on your fiftieth birthday, a golden golf ball for the man who has it all. It was signed: Your friend always, Peter.* How did the young man get this ball? I had given it to my former golfing partner, Julian Mantle, a few years ago. Julian had been a legend in the business world and one of the few friends I had been able to keep over the years. A man with an absolutely brilliant mind, he was widely acknowledged as one of the finest lawyers in the country. Unlike me, he had come from money, his grandfather being a prominent senator and his father, a highly respected judge of the federal court. Groomed for success at an early age, Julian graduated number one in his class at Harvard Law School and then landed a coveted position with a spectacularly successful law firm.

He rose to national prominence within a few short years, and his blue-chip client list included multibillion-dollar corporations, major sports teams, and even foreign governments. In his heyday, he managed a team of eighty-five talented lawyers and won a string of legal victories, which, to this day, causes me to marvel.

With an income well into the seven figures, he had everything anyone could want: a mansion in a tony neighborhood favored by celebrities, a private jet, a summer home on a tropical island, and his most prized possession of all — a shiny red Ferrari parked in the center of his driveway. But, like me, Julian had his flaws.

He worked like a fiend, regularly working through the night and then catching a few hours of sleep on the couch in his princely corner office before beginning the daily grind all over again. Although I loved playing golf with him, he was hardly ever available. I mostly heard the same excuse from his executive assistant: "I'm sorry, Mr. Franklin, Mr. Mantle will not be able to join you for golf this week due to an emergency that has come up on one of his cases. He does apologize." The man pushed himself relentlessly and, over time, lost most of his friends along with his once sympathetic wife.

I honestly thought Julian had a death wish or something. Not only did he work far too hard, he *lived* far too hard. He was well known for his late-night visits to the city's finest restaurants with sexy young fashion models, and for his reckless drinking escapades with a rowdy band of cronies, which often ended up in fights that were splashed across the newspapers the next day. Despite his statements to the contrary, Julian Mantle was digging himself into an early grave. I knew it, the lawyers at his firm knew it, and, deep within his soul, I think he knew it.

I watched Julian's steady decline with a feeling of sadness. At the age of fifty-three, he looked as if he was in his late seventies. The constant stress and strain of his hard-driving lifestyle wreaked havoc on him physically, transforming his face into a mass of wrinkles. The late-night dinners in expensive French restaurants, smoking thick Cuban cigars, and drinking cognac after cognac had left him embarrassingly overweight, and he constantly complained that he was sick and tired of being sick and tired. Over time, he lost his once wicked sense of humor and rarely laughed. A time eventually came when he stopped playing golf, even though I knew he loved the sport as well as our outings together. With all the work on his plate, Julian even stopped calling me. I knew he needed my friendship as much as I welcomed his, but I guess he just didn't care.

Then tragedy struck the Great Julian Mantle. One Monday morning, in the middle of the packed courtroom where Julian was arguing a case for one of his best corporate clients, Air Atlantic, he collapsed. Amid the frenzied screams of his paralegal and the clicking cameras of the media that were present, Julian was rushed to the hospital. On arrival, he was diagnosed as having suffered a massive heart attack and was rushed into the coronary care unit. The cardiologist said Julian was as close to death as any patient he had ever seen. But somehow he survived. The doctors said Julian was a fighter and seemed to have "a heroic will to live."

That sad episode changed Julian profoundly. The very next day, he announced he was leaving the practice of law for good. I'd heard through the grapevine that Julian had headed off to India on some kind of expedition. He told one of his partners he needed some answers and hoped he would find them in that ancient land that had, over the centuries, gathered such great wisdom. In a striking act of closure, Julian had sold his mansion, his jet, and his private island. However, it was his final gesture before departing that was his most unexpected: *Julian sold the Ferrari that he loved so much.*

My thoughts quickly returned to the young stranger in the monk's robes, now standing in the center of my office, still smiling and still wearing the hood over a thick mop of brown hair. "How did you get this gold-plated golf ball?" I asked in a quiet tone. "I gave this to a dear friend of mine a few years ago as a gift for a very special birthday."

"I know you did," replied the visitor. "And he really appreciated your gesture."

"And might I ask how you would know that?" I persisted.

"Because I'm the dear friend. I am Julian Mantle."

CHAPTER THREE

The Miraculous Transformation of a Corporate Warrior

I WAS ASTONISHED by what I had just heard. Could this young man in the peak of health really be Julian Mantle, a man who had fallen from the pinnacle of greatness as no one I have ever known? And if it *was* him, how could he possibly have undergone such a stunning change in appearance? I knew Julian had sold his mansion, his summer home, and even given up his prized red Ferrari. I knew he'd given up the trappings of the corporate world and trekked off to the Himalayas on some fanatical mission to seek answers to the deep questions he was struggling with. But surely a simple visit to that ancient and mystical place could not have so profoundly transformed a man who had all but worked himself into the ground.

Disturbed by the bizarre scenario that had just unfolded before me, my mind began to race to some of the other possibilities. Perhaps this was a prank masterminded by one of my less-than-mature managers to inject a little levity into what was sure to be a tension-filled week? Or maybe the young man was an infiltrator from a competitor seeking to get inside our operation to see how bad things really were? Perhaps this visitor in monk's clothing was a deranged trespasser out to seriously harm me. But before I could examine these options more fully, the young man spoke.

"Peter, I know it's hard for you to believe it's really me. I'd feel exactly the same way if I were in your shoes. All I'm asking from you is a little faith, a little bit of belief in life's small miracles. There's a purpose to my visit."

"And what might that be?" I asked, still not certain who was standing before me.

"Frankly, I've heard you are in big trouble and I've come to help. If what I've heard about GlobalView since my return from the Himalayas is true, you cannot afford not to listen to what I've come to tell you. I've discovered information that will return you and your business to the heights of success you once enjoyed. I've been given knowledge that will lead you to certain market leadership. I've learned lessons that will show you how to have the most loyal, dedicated, and inspired employees of any company in your field. This information was given to me by a very learned teacher, whom I met high in the mountains. The timeless wisdom he shared with me is not widely known here in the West. Yet it is so potent and so very profound that I am certain it will revolutionize your entire organization and do wonders for your bottom line."

"Go on," I replied, my curiosity piqued.

"The wisdom I've come to share with you is contained within a unique and extremely powerful system, a leadership blueprint of sorts. It's actually foolproof. Follow the system and then just sit back and watch your company return to prime health. Well, actually, it's designed to do far more than that. If you follow the formula with conviction, your business will be much more successful than it ever was. It will improve it in ways you never could have imagined. Morale and productivity will soar. Your people will be more committed and creative than you've ever seen them. They will be much more responsive and adaptive to change. Your team will start to work together again and deeply care about the work it is doing. And, to state the obvious, profits will go through the roof."

"Okay. You've got my attention," I responded. "But first let me ask you something. Assuming you are Julian, and that's quite an assumption, why are you dressed like a monk? The Julian Mantle I knew wouldn't be caught dead in anything less than Armani."

"Fair question, my friend," the young man replied with a mischievous grin, which, I quickly realized, looked very much like the one Julian was so well known for in his younger years. "Mind if I start my explanation at the beginning?"

"I'm all ears," I replied, leaning back into my plush leather chair for what I sensed would be a good story.

The young man proceeded to relate, in minute detail, the rise and fall of the legendary Julian Mantle, from his days as a brilliant young student at Harvard Law School to his unparalleled success as a litigation lawyer handling some of the most complex corporate law cases in the country. He spoke candidly of his victories and also of his well-documented decline. He talked about his dreams, his fears, his failed marriage, and his heart attack. He even referred to the intricacies of my golf game and said that he sorely missed our fun-filled afternoons in the sun.

"They were pretty great," I interrupted, sensing that, some-how, this young stranger dressed in the attire of the sages, really might be my long-lost friend Julian Mantle. Who else could have known all these details? I sat there silently, unsure of what to say next. Then I stood up and walked over to him.

"Julian, it really is you, isn't it?" I asked apologetically.

"Yes, it is. And it's really great to see you after all these years. That golf ball you gave me for my fiftieth really meant a lot to me."

I was delighted to see him. We embraced as only old friends can and began to revisit memories of our glory days together. But, in the back of my mind, one thought still nagged at me. I still couldn't find a rational explanation for Julian's amazing youthfulness.

Feeling my unease, Julian asked with his trademark flair, "A little curious to discover my beauty secrets?" His lips curved into a full grin.

"Stop teasing me, Julian. First you show up unannounced after all these years wearing that foolish-looking robe, bouncing rocks off my office window and scaring the daylights out of me on what has already been a stressful day. Then you stun me by telling me who you are and that you can offer me some priceless wisdom that will somehow save my bleeding company. And now you won't even explain how you managed to knock years off the way you look. You're walking a fine line, Julian," I said in mock annoyance.

"After my heart attack, I decided to make some drastic changes. I'm sure you heard that I sold the mansion and the summer home and the rest of my toys."

"At least you could have kept your Ferrari, Julian. That was such an amazing machine. I still remember seeing you fly around with that blonde bombshell you used to date in the passenger seat, her long hair waving through the wind."

Julian smiled for an instant. "The one with those hot pink miniskirts?"

"That's the one."

Then he grew pensive and serious. "I had to cut every tie I had to my former world if I really wanted to get somewhere new. I loved the Ferrari, but I knew it had to go. Otherwise it would have been like trying to go on a sailing adventure but hoping to keep a little rope tied to the dock for security. It just wouldn't work. So I sold everything that symbolized my hard-driving, 'take-no-prisoners' lifestyle and headed for India, a land I had always suspected was rich in knowledge and truth."

Julian then described how he trekked across that vast country in search of information he could use to improve the way he worked and lived. Sometimes he traveled by train, sometimes by bicycle or by foot. He visited ancient temples and studied under respected teachers. He met others who were also searching for answers to life's larger questions and made friendships that have lasted until this day. But during his first months in India, the wisdom he sought eluded him. Then, as he searched deeper and deeper, he began to hear whispers of a band of monks living high in the Himalayas.

According to legend, these sages, known only as the Great Sages of Sivana — Sivana meaning "oasis of enlightenment" in the language of their culture — had developed an extraordinary system that could be used to attain remarkable levels of personal and professional fulfillment. The only problem was that no one knew how to find these monks.

"Many people had tried to find them," said Julian. "Business people searched for them to discover their deep insights for leadership in the world of commerce. Others sought them for their lessons on leadership in life. But the higher reaches of the Himalayas are deadly, and many innocent lives were lost in pursuit of those elusive sages."

Never one to be deterred from a challenge, Julian threw caution to the wind and started climbing himself, determined to find what he was looking for. For many days and nights, he climbed those majestic mountains, beginning first at the moderate foothills and progressing to steeper and steeper paths that he prayed would lead him to the home of the Great Sages. He told me that he used that time in solitude to reflect on what his life had been — and all that it could be.

"In the corporate world, I had been so busy being busy, I never had time to think about life. And yet reflection and contemplation are among the most important of all business skills. I've since realized that in this information-led world we live in, ideas are the commodity of success, and the most effective people are the most effective thinkers," Julian observed. "My time alone in those mountains was transformational. For the first time in my life, Peter, I began to develop a true sense of self and to understand who I really was."

As he progressed on his trek, he grew weary and began to fear that he would succumb to the treacherous terrain as so many hope-filled adventurers before him. Then came a breakthrough. As he was traveling on a particularly steep path one sun-soaked morning, he caught a glimpse of another figure, dressed strangely in a long, flowing red robe topped by a dark blue hood. It had taken him many days to reach this stage and Julian was astonished to see another person. As he was many miles away from civilization and still unsure where Sivana lay, he called out to his fellow traveler.

The figure refused to respond and accelerated along the path, not even giving Julian the courtesy of a backward glimpse. Soon the mysterious traveler was running at full speed, the red robe dancing gracefully like crisp cotton sheets hanging from a clothesline on a windy autumn day.

"Please, friend, I need your help to find Sivana. I'm looking for the sages," yelled Julian. "I've been traveling for seven days with little food or water. I think I'm lost!"

The figure then stopped abruptly. As Julian approached, the traveler, whose face was hidden by the hood, remained strikingly still. Suddenly, a burst of sunlight struck the face, revealing that the traveler was a man. But the worldly wise Julian Mantle had never seen a man quite like this one. Although he guessed he was in his late fifties, his olive complexion was supple and smooth. His body appeared strong and powerful and the man radiated vitality and vigor. And his eyes were so penetrating that Julian said he was forced to look away.

"It didn't take me long to realize that I had found one of the elusive Sages of Sivana," said Julian, clearly still excited by this discovery, despite the passage of time. "So I poured my heart out to him on that mountain. I told him why I was there and what I hoped to learn. I told him of my former life in the corporate world, of my heart attack, and of my longing to find the secrets for true leadership in business and in life. I pleaded with him to take me to his people and to allow me to discover their wisdom for myself."

After listening intently to Julian's tale, the man put an arm on his shoulder and said gently, "If you truly have a heartfelt desire to learn the wisdom of a better way, then it is my duty to help you. I am indeed one of those sages you have come so far in search of. You are the first person to find us in many years. Congratulations. I admire your tenacity. You must have been quite a lawyer. If you like, you may come with me, as my guest, to our temple. It rests in a hidden part of this mountain region, still many hours away from here. My brothers and sisters will welcome you with open arms. We will work together to teach you the ancient principles and strategies that our ancestors have passed down through the ages."

There was, however, one condition the sage imposed upon Julian. "Before I take you into our private world and share our collective knowledge, I must request one promise from you. Although we are isolated here in these magical mountains, we are acutely aware of the turmoil your world is in. Leaders of every sort are struggling to cope with the great transition and tremendous turbulence that this new era of business has brought with it. Competition has never been so fierce, the rate of change has never been so high, and morale is plummeting as people struggle to find solid ground. With all this upheaval, people no longer have a sense of loyalty to their companies. They lack any connection to their work. Sadly, too many men and women fail to attach any meaning to what they do and that, in turn, has led to a lack of fulfillment in their lives. Your heart attack was personal evidence of this. But there is hope for these people, and the hope will come from you."

"How will the hope come from me?" Julian asked. "I'm here to learn from you."

"Don't worry," replied the sage. "While you are with us, here in these mystical mountains, you will discover a remarkable system for true leadership. We will show you a formula that any leader in the business world can immediately apply to transform the effectiveness of his of her company, raising it to far greater levels of prosperity and contribution. We will also teach you timeless truths for personal leadership so that you can get your own life back together and start making a real difference in the way you live. Few in this world have the privilege of learning the leadership wisdom you are about to acquire. And yet it is so important that it be made available to all. So, before I take you into our culture and introduce you to my brothers and sisters, I must place one requirement on you."

The sage then requested that Julian share the lessons he would learn at the feet of the Great Sages of Sivana with all those in the West who needed to hear them. It would be his duty to be the human conduit of the ancient wisdom of the sages, spreading it throughout this part of the world and transforming many lives in the process. Julian instantly accepted the sage's terms and promised he would carry their message to the West with sincerity and dedication.

"Don't tell me," I interjected with foresight. "I'm one of the people who needs to hear the message of the sages."

"Believe me, Peter, you will be glad you did. Neither you nor your company will ever be the same."

Brushing aside my usual skepticism, I replied with uncharacteristic enthusiasm, "When can we start?"

I guess I was simply fed up with the lack of progress we were making and hoped that Julian really could deliver the blueprint for renewal and transformation that were desperately needed. In spite of his many failings, there was one thing all who knew Julian Mantle could agree upon: he always told the truth.

"How about tomorrow afternoon? Is 5:00 P.M. okay?" Julian asked as he reached into his robe with his right hand.

"I had a meeting scheduled with one of our strategic partners, but I'll change it. Of course 5:00 P.M. is fine, Your Holiness," I replied mockingly. "Should we meet here? You seem to have a fondness for my rose garden. And security already knows you."

"Actually, I had another place in mind. Let's meet at our old golf club. There's something I need to show you, and that place will be perfect."

He then pulled out from his robe what appeared to be a small wooden piece of a jigsaw puzzle and, as he had done with the gold ball that had emerged from it earlier, he tossed it into the air for me to catch.

After giving me a quick smile, he turned around and walked past the security guards who had been sipping coffee in the hallway outside my door. "See you tomorrow," I heard, Julian's voice trailing off.

As I watched the long red robe of my former golf partner swing from side to side as he moved farther down the long corridor that led to the exit, I shook my head in disbelief. I felt a sense of excitement I had not had in a long time. Perhaps there was hope for GlobalView after all. Perhaps I would be able to get my troops inspired and rejuvenated again. Perhaps I could actually regain a clear sense of vision for the future of this once-great organization. Maybe this special leadership system Julian had discovered in the Himalayas would allow us to seize the opportunities the new marketplace presented and experience far greater success than we had ever known. And maybe I'd finally learn how Julian had transformed himself.

As I caught myself staring at the foot-high pile of paperwork on my desk, I turned away to study the wooden jigsaw piece that Julian had tossed to me. I noticed it had a design on it. Although I looked closely, I could not figure out what it was. But I did notice that there were also words carved into the wood. *How strange*, I thought. The words were almost illegible, having worn down with the passage of time. I quickly reached into the drawer of my desk and pulled out a magnifying glass. Finally, I could read the words. They read simply, *Ritual 1: Link Paycheck to Purpose.*

CHAPTER FOUR

❧

The Wisdom of Leadership Vision

Of all of the beautiful truths pertaining to the soul which have been restored and brought to light in this age, none is more gladdening or fruitful of divine promise and confidence than this — that you are the master of your thought, the molder of your character, and the maker and shaper of condition, environment and destiny.

James Allen

MY HEART WAS RACING as I turned onto the tree-lined country road that would eventually lead me to my golf club, a club widely recognized as one of the most prestigious in the entire country. Judges, senators, financiers, and celebrities were well represented among the membership, and a ten-year waiting list ensured that this would remain the case for the foreseeable future. I felt lucky to be able to belong to such an establishment. I would have felt even luckier if I'd had the time to enjoy the facility on a more regular basis. With all

31

the turmoil GlobalView was facing, a round of golf was nothing more than a fantasy.

As I approached the clubhouse, a massive wooden structure with majestic pillars and a breathtaking view of the beautifully manicured golf course and the lush gardens that surrounded it, I spotted Julian. He was sitting up on the verandah, his table shaded by an umbrella to protect him from the late afternoon sun. He appeared to be reading a book as he sipped his drink. And, in violation of the club's rigid dress code, he still had on his ruby red robe. I couldn't help but smile. Julian always did things his own way. And you had to love him for it.

"Julian," I called out, as I got out of my car and walked up the stairs that led to the veranda.

As he saw me approaching, he stood up and extended his hand. "Thanks for coming, Peter. I promise you won't be disappointed."

As we settled in, I ordered a martini. It had been another rough day at the office, and I felt that the drink would help me unwind. I had been under such pressure over the past few months that anything that would calm my nerves was welcome. "What are you reading?" I asked, looking down at the leather-bound book Julian held in his hand.

"It's a book on the life of Gandhi."

"I didn't know you were into Gandhi. As a matter of fact, I can't recall seeing you carry around a book in all the years I've known you."

"I have nothing in common with the time-starved, over-stressed Julian Mantle that you once knew. I've changed in so many ways you cannot imagine. One of the many lessons I learned in the Himalayas is that with the twin elements of knowledge and courage, all things are possible. So I now make sure that I read from a good book every single day. Doing so connects me to the intelligence I need and keeps me focused on where I'm going. And inspired by the knowledge of where I'm going, I maintain the courage to keep moving forward."

"Interesting. But why Gandhi?"

"Since my time with the sages, I've become a serious student of leadership. When most people hear the word *leadership*, they think of it only in the business context. They imagine leaders of companies, inspiring their followers to be more productive and committing themselves to their grand visions of the future. But the sages taught me that leadership is really much broader than that. *Leadership is really a philosophy for life.* While CEOs and managers can be great leaders, so can caring teachers, committed scientists, and compassionate mothers. Coaches lead sports teams and politicians lead communities. And it all begins from within, by having the self-discipline to lead and know yourself. To understand that the essence of your life lies in leadership. As Robert Louis Stevenson once said, 'To be what we are, and to become what we are capable of becoming, is the only end of life.'

"Truly wise people aim, not only for leadership in their businesses but also within their lives. And so, since I've returned from the Himalayas, I've been studying the life of Gandhi, a man whom I believe to have been one of the greatest all-around leaders ever to have graced the earth. He had the wisdom to lead his people in the direction of his future vision, but he also had the courage to lead himself and live with great character. He is a model of enlightened and effective leadership."

"That's hard to disagree with."

"One day Gandhi was getting off a train when one of his shoes slipped off and onto the track. As the train had started to move, he could not retrieve it, so he did something that startled his companions."

"Which was?"

"He removed his other shoe and threw it near where the first one sat. His companions immediately asked for an explanation. As he walked shoeless down the platform, he smiled gently and replied, 'Now, the poor man who finds the shoe lying on the track will have a pair he can use.' "

"Wow."

"Gandhi also had an abundance of humility, a great leadership quality if there ever was one."

"Really? I never would have thought humility was that important."

"Oh, but it is," Julian replied as he gently called over a passing waiter and ordered a cup of herbal tea. Within minutes, the waiter had returned with a teapot and an elegant china teacup for Julian. Julian then started to pour the tea into the cup. He poured until the cup was full, but then, most oddly, he kept on pouring! Soon the tea spilled across the table onto the deck of the veranda. And yet he continued to pour.

"Julian, what are you trying to prove?" I asked incredulously.

"An essential leadership lesson," he replied calmly. "Most leaders are a lot like this teacup."

"How so?"

"Well, just like this cup, they are full to the brim. They have filled their minds so full of their opinions, ideas, and biases that nothing new can get in. And in our rapidly changing world, where leaders must constantly be learning new concepts and equipping themselves with new skills, that's a deadly character flaw."

"So what's the solution?"

"It's simple. They must *empty their cups*. They must constantly be receptive to new knowledge. They must always view themselves as lifelong students, no matter how many initials and titles follow their names on their upscale business cards. They must adopt what the sages of the East refer to as the Beginner's Mind, an essential attitude for every leader destined for success. They must grow humble. That's why I say that humility is a fundamental leadership discipline. And this is why I have come to admire Gandhi."

Julian continued, oblivious to the stares he was attracting from the other members who had come up to the verandah to relax after a round of golf. "The sage I told you about yesterday, the one I met while I was climbing along the mountain, was the nominal leader of the Great Sages of Sivana. After I accepted his condition and promised I would spread their system for leadership through the West, he introduced himself as Yogi Raman and led me along a series of intricate mountain paths that eventually led to a lush green valley. On one side of the valley stood the towering snow-capped Himalayas, majestically reaching high against the clear blue sky. The other sides were guarded by a thick forest of pine trees that spilled their fragrance throughout the valley. Yogi Raman smiled at me and said, 'Welcome to the Nirvana of Sivana.'

"We then descended along another narrow path that took us deep into the forest. I still remember being powerfully affected by the smell of the pine and sandalwood that passed through the air of that otherworldly place. On the forest floor were richly colored orchids and other exotic flowers, the likes of which I had never seen before. Suddenly, I began to hear other voices as we approached a clearing. As we grew nearer, I caught a glimpse of a sight I can assure you I will never forget as long as I live."

"What did you see?" I asked.

Robin Sharma

"Before me stood an entire village made solely from what appeared to be roses. At the center of the village was a tiny temple, the kind I had seen on my visits to Thailand and Nepal. But this temple was made of red, white, and pink flowers, held together with long strands of multicolored string and twigs. Surrounding the temple was a series of small huts, apparently the simple homes of the monks.

"Even more astonishing were the inhabitants themselves," Julian added. "The men wore the same red-robed uniform that Yogi Raman was wearing and smiled gently as they passed by. Their expressions conveyed a deep sense of serenity and their eyes a deep sense of wisdom. Rather than growing agitated at the sight of an unexpected visitor who had broken the sanctity of their mountain hideaway, they quietly bowed their heads and then continued to perform the tasks they had been working at. The women were equally impressive. Wearing beautiful pink silk saris that flowed to the ground and with their shiny black hair adorned by bright white lotuses, they moved gracefully through the village. I had never seen people like this before. Even though they were all mature adults, each one of them radiated joy, their eyes twinkling as an expression of their vitality and passion for life. Not one of them had wrinkles. Not one of them had gray hair. Not one of them looked old. I was speechless."

Julian told me that Yogi Raman then showed him to his living quarters, a small hut that would serve as his home for the next few months.

"Let's head down to the fairway," said Julian, standing up. "I'll continue with my story as we walk. And bring along those golf clubs," he requested, motioning toward what appeared to be a well-worn set that someone had apparently forgotten on the veranda.

36

"Are you actually going to try and play a round in those robes?"

"No, there's something much more important I want to show you."

As we walked toward the golf course, Julian continued to share his amazing tale with me. Sensing his burning desire to learn the sages' leadership wisdom, Yogi Raman took Julian under his tutelage. He spent literally every waking hour with his eager student, happily sharing his accumulated knowledge and instructing Julian on how to apply it. On some days they would rise with the sun and spend hours discussing the timeless truths that Yogi Raman had offered, Julian's quick legal mind delighting in this powerful information he knew would change his life along with the lives of so many others in his part of the world. On other days, they would walk silently in the pine forest, enjoying the gift of each other's presence while savoring the opportunity to reflect on the philosophies they had been discussing.

In time, the sage became more like a father to Julian than a teacher. He showed Julian how to see his life in a whole new perspective and truly liberate the fullness of his personal potential. Knowing of Julian's brush with death after years of neglecting his health, Yogi Raman initially focused on teaching Julian an extremely powerful self-management and life-improvement process that would transform the way he looked and felt.

The sage told Julian that "inner leadership precedes outer leadership," and before he could come to understand the time-honored dynamics of leading others, he had to understand how to lead himself. So Yogi Raman taught him little-known skills to manage stress, break his worry habit, and simplify his life. He taught him how to enhance his energy levels, unblock his creativity, and unleash his vitality. Within a number of weeks, Julian had undergone both an outer and inner metamorphosis. He looked years younger, was full of strength, and felt more positive about his future than he had in many years. He actually began to believe he could do anything, be anything, and make a real difference in the world by spreading the priceless wisdom he had discovered. The ancient lessons of the Great Sages of Sivana had started to work their miracles.

With his student returned to a splendid state of physical and psychological health, Yogi Raman began to share the leadership system Julian had promised would revolutionize GlobalView and allow it to reach a world-class level of achievement and effectiveness.

"This wise leader of the Great Sages of Sivana believed that all failure, whether in the business world or in one's personal life, could ultimately be traced back to a failure in leadership. Companies don't perform at their peak when their leaders are unskilled and unwise. People don't perform at their best when they have no leadership over their lives. He told me that although he lived in an isolated part of the world, he knew there was what he called 'a leadership crisis' in our part of the world. Yogi Raman said he held the solution."

"I've spent a lifetime reflecting on the elements of enlightened leadership," Julian remembered the sage telling him one afternoon as they relaxed in a mountain meadow after exploring and hiking in that surreal place. "I've devoted many years to silently contemplating what made the greatest leaders so great. As a monk, I have pledged allegiance to the truth. So my life has been dedicated to searching for truths of leadership. Over time, I have come to understand that the most influential and respected leaders aligned their leadership with certain ancient laws. I've structured these laws into an extremely effective system for dynamic leadership, a blueprint of sorts that will help any leader realize his or her professional and personal potential. Now I shall share what I have learned with you."

"And what did Yogi Raman tell you?" I asked intently, as we finally reached the barren golf course.

"He told me that the most enlightened, dynamic, and effective leaders all possessed one quality that the lesser ones lacked."

"And that quality is?"

"I think it would be better if I demonstrated it." Julian then reached into the leather golf bag I was carrying and pulled out a club.

"You're not going to tell me you also worked on your golf game while you studied under the sages!"

"Actually, I did. I played golf every single day. It was very therapeutic and greatly contributed to my recovery."

"Really," I said in disbelief. "And I suppose these magical monks had also developed a world-class golf resort in the middle of their mountain hideaway so they could play a few rounds to break up the monotony of their days? Probably had little bamboo golf carts to whiz them from hole to hole, did they?"

"Very funny," Julian replied, taking my sarcasm in stride. What else could he expect? His story was moving from the bizarre to the incredible. "No, I actually played golf in my mind, Peter."

"I've never heard that one before."

"A few years ago, I remember reading a magazine article about a Vietnam vet who managed to survive his days in solitary confinement by playing imaginary games of chess. Not only did this help him pass the time, it also dramatically improved his playing ability. By the time he got out and had the opportunity to play with a real opponent on a real board, his chess skills had become nothing short of brilliant."

"Amazing."

"I felt exactly the same way when I heard about that story, Peter. So when, in some of my quieter moments among the sages, I began to reflect on how much I had loved playing golf in my younger years, I decided I would model the war veteran's strategy and practice playing golf in my mind. I had enjoyed the game so much as a kid, I thought it would greatly assist my recovery."

"Did it make a difference in your golf game?"

"I don't know. This is the first time I've been on a golf course in years. Actually, I think the last time I played was with you. But I've probably played over a thousand rounds in my mind, so I don't really feel like I've been away from the game at all. Okay, watch closely now. I think what you're about to see might surprise you."

Julian then reached into his robe and pulled out the gold-plated golf ball that I'd returned to him.

"You're not going to use that one, are you? Do you have any idea how much that cost me, Julian?" I asked, mildly irritated that my friend would use my special birthday present to him in his demonstration.

"Watch closely," was the only reply I received as he focused intently on the hole at the other end of the fairway, his ultimate destination. Then with the ease and grace of a seasoned professional, he swung the club, striking the ball perfectly and sending it soaring high into the air. I'd never seen Julian hit the ball like that. However, in spite of his shot, it appeared as if the ball would fall short of its target. I looked at him and gave him my best "nice-try" expression.

Then something unbelievable happened. The ball seemed to speed up in the air, as if it had been blessed with the support of a convenient gust of wind. It now sped precisely toward its intended destination. A couple of groundskeepers, who had witnessed this display, had quickly taken off their hats so as not to miss seeing where the ball would land. Even a few of the golfers relaxing on the clubhouse veranda were leaning over the railing to see what would happen.

The ball then dropped down from the sky onto the green next to the first hole and began to roll slowly but directly toward it. No golfer had shot a hole-in-one on this course for quite some time, but perhaps my friend, adorned in the robe of a traditional monk and wearing nothing on his feet but his faithful sandals, would be the first to end this drought. The ball kept on inching toward the hole. Then it seemed to stop.

"Oh, Julian," I said, in sincere disappointment. "So close and yet so far."

"Just wait, Peter. One of the leadership lessons I've learned is that *immediately before a great victory, one will often experience some form of difficulty. The key is to maintain your focus and keep on believing.*"

Then, just when it appeared to all that the ball had come to rest, it rolled the remaining two inches and dropped into the hole.

"Hurrah!" one of the groundskeepers shouted at the top of his lungs after witnessing this extraordinary event. Julian threw his fists into the air and began to do a little dance, obviously delighted by his achievement.

I simply laughed and shook my head. "Wow, Julian. You never cease to amaze me! Congratulations!"

After regaining my composure, I asked Julian how he did it. "Did you actually intend to shoot a hole-in-one?"

"I did. But to be honest, I wasn't certain it would happen. I'd rehearsed that very shot on this very course hundreds of times in my mind when I was up in the Himalayas. It began to be a game

I would play, just to keep my imagination sharp. I had great fun doing it. I must admit that even I'm a little surprised that my mental training produced such a fabulous result. But the fact that it worked proves the important point I brought you down here to make," offered Julian with a hint of mystery.

"Does it have something to do with the piece of the puzzle you gave me yesterday?"

"Yes, it does. Let me ask you this question, Peter. What do you think allowed me to shoot a hole-in-one the first time I stepped on a golf course after so many years?"

"Well, I think you answered the question yourself, Julian. It was because of your mental rehearsals during the time you were up in the Himalayas. You practiced doing what you just did so many times that you must have created something similar to a blueprint in your mind. Then you came down here today and, against the odds, translated that mental blueprint into reality."

"Very good, Peter. You always had a quick mind and clearly understand the process I followed. I'm impressed."

"You know I love the game of golf and will do anything to shave a couple of strokes off my game. So, over the past few months, I've been reading a lot of books on the lives and lessons of the world's greatest golfers. If there was one thing they all agreed on, it was that 'golf is a mental game.' Jack Nicklaus, for example, mentioned that after walking the course he was about to play, he would envision the shots he hoped to make hundreds of times in his mind's eye. This became his secret advantage. So when you told me you did the same thing, it really didn't come as such a surprise."

"And the greatest leaders in the world of business do the same thing," Julian stated.

"They all visualize their golf shots?" I replied with a grin.

"No, Peter. They clearly envision their future paths in the present moment. They manufacture a crystal-clear blueprint or picture of what their companies will look like in the coming years. They know intimately the exact nature of the success they and their people are striving for. And every step they take is designed to move them closer to their vividly imagined future. In a word, my friend, they have a *vision* that inspires them to reach for the stars. That is the ultimate secret of their greatness as leaders."

"It seems so simple. Just clearly envision my company's future and I'll become a great leader?" I queried.

"I didn't mean to suggest that it was that simple. There are many more leadership practices and philosophies followed by enlightened, high-performing leaders that allow them to lead as they do. Yogi Raman taught them all to me and I assure you I will soon share them with you. But, for now, just remember that *great organizations begin with great leaders. And every great leader has bold dreams.* Effective leaders are visionaries who craft clear pictures of their companies' futures and then link them to the present activities of the people they are leading. In this way, all actions have a purpose: to bring the organizations closer to the result imagined by their leaders. It's just like Woodrow Wilson said, 'You are not here to merely make a living. You are here in order to enable the world to live more amply, with greater vision, with a finer spirit of hope and achievement. You are here to enrich the world, and you impoverish yourself if you forget that errand.' "

"So well said."

"And remember, once you surrender to your vision, success begins to chase you. Ultimately, you really can't pursue success, success ensues. It flows as the unintended by-product of effective efforts concentrated in the direction of a worthy purpose."

"Yogi Raman, a monk living high in the Himalayas, taught you that?" I queried.

"Yogi Raman spent many years studying the fundamentals of leadership by studying the lives of history's greatest leaders. He shared with me a timeless system that anyone in a leadership position can use to inspire and energize his or her team into action and raise the organization to heights previously unimagined. Yogi Raman might not have known all the complexities of the modern world of business here in the West, but he didn't need to. The wisdom he shared with me is based on ancient leadership truths that have been passed down through the centuries. These truths could also be characterized as immutable laws since, like the laws of nature, they have stood the test of time and will continue to do so. And while the world of business is drowning in a sea of change, these truths for leading people are not."

"So every great leader is a visionary. He or she has made a clear connection to the future by vividly imagining an end result. It's kind of like what Henry Kissinger was quoted as saying in the paper a few years back: 'The task of the leader is to get his people from where they are to where they have never been.' Is that an accurate way to summarize what you are telling me?"

"Yes, it is, Peter. You seem to have grasped the concept well—perfectly, actually. But I'll offer you another example anyway. Do you remember that famous eye surgeon we used to play golf with from time to time?"

"Sure. I really liked the guy. He had a wonderful sense of humor."

"That's him. He also used to organize that annual gala dinner and dance for all the ophthalmologists in the city. Remember what he named it?"

"How could I forget?" I replied with a grin. "The Eye Ball."

"Well, one afternoon, we were out on the course and I remember him telling me about one of his very young patients who suffered from a medical condition known as amblyopia. Apparently, another doctor had mistakenly put a patch over the child's good eye rather than the one that needed protection. After the patch was taken off, it was discovered, to the surprise and sadness of all concerned, that the little boy had completely lost the sight in that good eye. Apparently, the eye covering had stunted the development of his vision and caused blindness. That's the phenomenon that the term *amblyopia* describes."

"Remarkable."

"I've never forgotten that story, Peter. I also think it applies to the leadership lesson I'm offering to you. In today's business world, too many leaders become creatures of habit. They do the same things in the same way with the same people every day. They rarely have new thoughts, generate fresh ideas, or take calculated risks. Instead, they confine their leadership to a secure area of comfort and refuse to leave it. Such leaders eventually suffer from their own form of amblyopia."

"How so?"

"By spending their days doing the same old things, it's like they've placed patches over their good eyes. They become unable to see the tremendous opportunities presented by these rapidly changing times. And, eventually, by not using their natural vision, they lose it and grow blind. Never let this happen to you, my friend. Take your blinders off and start looking for new opportunities. *The best way to succeed in the future is to create it.* As Helen Keller once said, 'I'd rather be blind than have sight without vision.'"

Julian continued. "Now that you understand that the most enlightened and effective leaders are 'visionary leaders,' my duty is to give you the tools and skills to help you become one. And this is where Yogi Raman's leadership system comes in."

"First, may I ask you a quick question?"

"Sure," Julian replied as we strolled back to the clubhouse.

"I really want to learn what you have to teach me. You know that GlobalView is in big trouble. My best programmers are jumping ship, morale has been destroyed, no one trusts management, and teamwork is a thing of the past. In an industry that demands relentless innovation, we seem to have lost our creative fire. And all the change that we are being forced to deal with is crippling my people. Technology is changing, the industry is changing, and our customers' expectations are changing. On top of all that, I just can't seem to figure out the direction in which the company needs to move."

I continued to share my frustrations with Julian. "What I'm really trying to tell you is that I know I need to improve my leadership abilities. At Digitech, I was promoted to higher and higher management positions. And though I went to a few leadership development courses here and there, in all those years, no one ever really took me aside and taught me how to lead people. No one ever showed me what to do to deeply motivate my team or communicate more effectively. No one explained how I could boost productivity while enhancing employee commitment. I've never even learned something as fundamental as the art of managing my time and getting things done.

"And now that I run my own company, it's even worse. I always seem to have far too much to do and too little time. Everyone expects me to have all the answers to all their questions. I'm constantly under stress and take out my frustration on my people, which only makes things worse. As for a sense of balance between my professional and personal life, it's just a dream. I say to myself, 'Next year will be the year I get back into shape or start spending more time with my family.' But things never seem to slow down. So, if you don't mind, I'm going to really take advantage of our time together and dig deep into the elements of great leadership. I want to ask you some of the basic questions I've always wanted to ask but never did, for fear of looking foolish."

"Please do," Julian replied gently.

"Okay. First of all, what does the word *leadership* really mean? What does it really stand for? Although I'm running a huge company with more than 2,500 employees, I've never really been able to pinpoint the meaning of the word."

"It's like I said before: leadership is all about focused action in the direction of a worthy purpose. Leadership is about realizing that the impossible is generally the untried. Many people think that a leader is the man or the woman with the title of CEO or president. Actually, leadership is not about position, it is about action. Your managers can be great leaders. Your programmers can be great leaders. The shop foreman down on the factory floor can be a great leader. You see, Peter, to lead is to inspire, energize, and influence. *Leadership is not about managing things but about developing people.* Visionary leaders are those who understand that the true assets of any organization go up the elevator in the morning and down it every night. Quite simply, leadership is about helping people to liberate the fullness of their talents while they pursue a vision you have helped them understand is a worthy and meaningful one. You can do this. Your managers can do this. Even your frontline workers can show leadership in the work that they do. And the truly effective leaders have to live in two places at once."

"I'm not sure I understand you."

"The best leaders recognize that leadership is a craft, not a gift. They constantly work to refine their art. And one of the things they work hardest to develop is an ability to be present-based but future-focused. Great leaders have mastered the twin skills of managing the present while, at the same time, inventing the future. That's why I say they have to live in two places at the same time. They need to live in the present and guide the improvement of current operations by enhancing quality, streamlining systems, and raising customer-care standards. But at the same time, they must create, shape, and nurture a clear blueprint for the future. Yogi Raman put it elegantly when he said, *'The visionary leader is one who has learned how to focus on the summit while clearing the path.'* A company without a fanatical commitment to refining operations will soon be surpassed by its competition. But a company without a strikingly clear ideal to work toward will soon be out of business."

"And is this where the piece of the jigsaw puzzle you left with me yesterday comes in?"

"Yes. Do you recall what the words on it said?" Julian asked.

Luckily, I had brought the piece with me and quickly lifted it from the front pocket of the yellow golf shirt I had on.

"I couldn't figure out what the design on it was, but I was able to read the words."

"Fine. And what did they say?"

"*Ritual 1: Link Paycheck to Purpose,*" I answered dutifully. "I'm not quite sure what that means, Julian."

"You will be before long."

RITUAL 1

❦

Link Paycheck to Purpose

❦

CHAPTER FIVE

The Ritual of a Compelling Future Focus

Life affords no higher pleasure than that of surmounting difficulties, passing from one stage of success to another, forming new wishes and seeing them gratified. He that labors in any great or laudable undertaking has his fatigues first supported by hope and afterwards supported by joy.

Samuel Johnson

WHILE JULIAN AND I had been chatting on the veranda, the sun had slowly set, making way for a peaceful yet particularly humid summer's evening. Despite the heat, he steadfastly refused to take off his robe. "I'm just fine," Julian replied courteously. "But I sure would appreciate a glass of ice water."

"With pleasure," I responded, quickly signaling the waiter to come over once again and informing him of my unusually attired guest's simple request. I had realized that Julian truly was a different man from the hard-living, stress-ridden corporate warrior he once was. Gone was the affinity for alcohol, recklessness, and profanity that had characterized his notorious lifestyle. He was a model of good health, good judgment, and a testament to the principles he was sharing.

"You know, Peter, there are a lot of so-called management gurus. They travel from city to city giving seminar after seminar and write book after book. While many of them develop useless buzzwords and jargon to justify their existences, the best ones really do have valuable ideas that would help improve organizations. The problem lies in what I call the Performance Gap. That's what prevents many businesses from reaching levels of greatness."

"The Performance Gap?"

"It's a theory that explains why knowledge generally doesn't translate into results. You see, all too often we know what we should do but we don't do what we know. We are human beings when what we really should be are humans *doing*. Many leaders know they should have a clear sense of their future vision and powerfully communicate it to the people they have the privilege to lead. They know they need to take steps to develop deeper connections with those under their leadership. The problem is that they have failed to develop the action habit. And, therefore, they put off doing what they intuitively know they should do. They spend their days majoring in minor things; and slowly the weeks, months, and years slip by them. These types of leaders never fully realize that 90 percent of leadership success comes in the follow-through, in the implementation and execution of the knowledge they have gathered. Everyone says we are so fortunate to live in this age of information. But what most people fail to appreciate is that information alone is not power. Power and competitive advantage come only when sound information is decisively acted upon."

"That's so true, Julian. Most of us in our company know at least a few dozen things we could probably implement in a week or so to at least improve the situation. And yet we are so busy with the daily emergencies that always seem to burden us that we end up putting off doing them until the next quarter and then the quarter after that."

"Quite right. So remember, as I share Yogi Raman's leadership wisdom with you, that the key to improving your leadership performance is to passionately act on it. Don't squirrel it away hoping you will have time down the road to study it and put it into play. Recognize its power and deeply embed it into your daily routine so that you practice its principles daily. Make it a part of your leadership and your life right now. Only then will you see quantum improvements in your effectiveness as a leader of people and in the productivity and performance of GlobalView. As noted by Herodotus so many years ago, 'This is the bitterest pain among men, to have much knowledge but no power.'"

"Any advice on how I might go about 'making the wisdom a part of my leadership and my life today,' as you suggest?"

"Most important of all, you must begin to *ritualize* the wisdom you are about to discover," Julian replied.

"Huh?"

"The best way to ensure these leadership lessons become a part of who you are is to create rituals around them. That is one of the most timeless and essential of all the leadership truths I will deliver to you."

"Can you give me an example of a ritual, just so I'm clear about what you're getting at?"

"Sure. One simple ritual the sages practiced with an almost obsessive sense of commitment was getting up at dawn. They felt this gave them a tremendous head start on their days and fostered self-discipline. By engaging in this simple practice every single day, it became a part of who they were. A time came when they couldn't have slept in even if they tried."

"One of my managers is the same way, Julian. As a boy, his father forced him to get up at 5:00 A.M. every single day of the week. He told him he was doing it for his own good, 'to build character.' Now, even if he's on vacation, he still gets up at that ungodly time of the day. Perhaps that's why he's one of the most productive people in our company."

"Personal productivity is generated in many ways. Getting up early is certainly one of the best of them. But the point I'm making is that both the Great Sages of Sivana and your top manager *ritualized* the discipline of getting up early. Other people have ritualized the discipline of exercising every lunchtime, and still others have ritualized the practice of reading every night. What I'm really trying to say, and this is so important for you to understand, is that the only way you will become a visionary leader and liberate the fullness of your leadership talents is by making the truths I'm about to reveal to you part of your daily routine. You need to make them iron-clad rituals, as all the visionary leaders before you have done. In this way you will move beyond simply knowing to doing."

"Could brushing your teeth be considered a ritual?" I asked earnestly.

"Definitely. Would you ever dream of going into the office without brushing your teeth?"

"I wouldn't dare inflict such pain on my staff, Julian," I replied with a hearty laugh, my first in a long time. "Cruel and unusual punishment has been banned in this part of the world, in case you forgot!"

Julian chuckled but then quickly returned to the point he was making. "You brush your teeth every single morning and wouldn't dream of not doing it. So it's a perfect example of a ritual. If you can integrate the leadership truths from Yogi Raman's system into your routine to the same degree, your success as a visionary leader will be guaranteed. This I promise you."

"Great, I'm feeling excited already. So far you've explained that enlightened and effective leaders all have a vividly imagined future vision. They know precisely where they want to go and concentrate their energies on getting there. You've also taught me that the leadership truths that make up Yogi Raman's timeless success system need to be made into rituals so that I practice them daily, almost unconsciously, in spite of how busy I get. Would it be possible for you to give me the elements of this ancient system now?" I asked, barely containing my curiosity.

Julian looked up to the sky, which had now grown dark and star-filled. He gazed for what seemed like an eternity at one star in particular, squinting his eyes in an effort to see it more clearly. Then he muttered something under his breath. While I couldn't make out all that he said, I did hear: "So there you are, my friend. I've missed you for a while."

Then, realizing that he had drifted off, he quickly caught himself and returned his attention to me, looking mildly embarrassed. "Sorry about that, Peter. When one spends as much time alone as I do, one's social graces tend to diminish. I apologize for my mind wandering off like that. It's just that I spotted something I haven't been able to find all week."

After a moment, he continued. "Yogi Raman taught me that there were a series of specific rituals practiced by visionary leaders, eight to be precise. These eight disciplines represented a distillation of all the leadership wisdom that had been passed down through the ages and practiced by the world's greatest leaders of people. These were not the quick-fix, flavor-of-the-month strategies that are so prevalent in today's businessplace. Instead, they reflected the ageless truths about how to deeply stir men and women into action, how to cultivate tremendous loyalty and respect, and how to bring out the very best in the people you lead. Yogi Raman, in all his brilliance, fashioned these eight rituals into the leadership system I've promised to share with you for some time now. You have been patient and sincere in your interest to learn a better way to lead. And so the time has come for me to teach the system to you."

"Would it be fair to assume that the piece of the puzzle you left with me yesterday after your surprise visit to my office has something to do with the first ritual of Yogi Raman's leadership system?"

"Indeed it does, Peter. The First Ritual of Visionary Leaders is Link Paycheck to Purpose. Simply put, this is the ritual of a compelling future focus. As I have already told you, all enlightened leaders have a richly imagined vision of their organization's future. But having a vision is not enough. The vision must excite the minds and touch the hearts of the men and women of your organization. People will go far beyond the call of duty when their leader paints for them a future vision that is compelling and important. *Purpose is the most powerful motivator in the world.*

"Yogi Raman told me that one of the greatest human hungers is the need we all have to make a difference in the lives of others. People have a deep inner need to be a part of something larger than themselves. Whether we are speaking of the CEO or the shipping clerk, every human being needs to feel that he or she is making some sort of contribution. Great leaders appreciate this hunger and constantly communicate to their followers how what they do in their daily work positively affects the world at large. They also fan the flames of excitement within their organizations by continually showing their people that the work they are doing is moving them closer to a compelling cause. To put it simply, these leaders give their followers a reason to get up in the morning."

"Very interesting. Any ideas on how I could apply this to my situation?"

"Earlier you said that low morale is stifling GlobalView's growth."

"True."

"Then remember this, Peter. There's no such thing as an unmotivated person, only an unmotivated employee. You can take any member of your team whom you believe lacks motivation and initiative and scrutinize his or her personal life, and guess what you'll see?"

"Dare I guess?"

"You will see that that person has hobbies that he loves. You will see that he has interests that excite him. You will discover that he works late into the night on his stamp collection or spends hours learning new languages or passionately playing musical instruments. Every single person on this planet has the ability to get excited and motivated about something. The leader's primary task is to get his team excited and motivated about the compelling cause that is his vision. Rather than constantly ordering your people to work toward the future goals you have developed, why not give them a reason to do so? And if you find that they are still unmotivated, understand that it is because you still have not given them enough reasons to buy into your picture of the future. Remember what the psychologists have known for many years:

human beings naturally move away from pain and toward pleasure. Visionary leaders find ways to associate pleasure with the daily work of their employees and the ultimate cause they are working toward. *They link paycheck to purpose.*"

Julian continued. "What's your current corporate mission statement?"

"C'mon, I'm tired of hearing about mission statements. I think that whole idea has been done to death, if you don't mind my saying so."

"I agree. But the fact remains that crafting a statement of your organization's future can only serve to refocus the energies of your people on the things that count. So bear with me, please."

"To be the preferred supplier of our customers, to create high-quality products, and to grow into a five-billion-dollar company within five years," I stated proudly.

"Do you truly think a mission statement like that will inspire people to give their best to the company? Do you seriously believe you have given your people a reason to get out of bed every morning? Have you really shown them a compelling cause they can work toward? Every company wants to be the customer's preferred supplier. And about the five billion dollars, I'll let you in on a secret. You're probably the only one in the entire company who is excited about that one. It has no *emotional* impact on the average person within the organization, working hard to pay off the mortgage and to put her kids through school."

Julian's words stung me. I knew he wanted to challenge me to explore new pathways of thought. But he was hitting pretty close to home. I had drawn up that mission statement myself. And it meant a lot to me.

"Let's look for ways to reframe your future vision to make it more compelling to those you lead. What business are you in?"

"We make software."

"And what is your primary market?"

"The health-care field. Our software is used primarily by major hospitals and health-care providers to better serve their patients."

"Ah, now we're getting somewhere," Julian replied. "And what exactly does your software allow your customers to do?"

"Well, our bestselling program assists doctors and nurses in the monitoring of critical-care patients. Although it was only developed last year, our industry trade magazine recently reported that that piece of software alone has saved over 100,000 lives."

"Now that's what I mean by a compelling cause," said Julian with great enthusiasm. "And what kind of revenue would GlobalView be generating if you were saving millions of lives?"

"That's really hard to say. There are so many factors that I'd have to consider and —"

"For the purposes of the point I'm trying to make, let's be very flexible with the numbers," Julian interrupted. "Just tell me, is it possible that if the software program you are selling saved millions and millions of lives each year, the revenues of your company could rise to five billion?"

"Yes, it's possible," I admitted.

"Fine, then. Imagine that your mission statement was amended to read, 'GlobalView is passionately committed to saving the lives of men, women, and children by providing our respected customers with cutting-edge, high-value software that allows them to brilliantly serve their patients' needs. Our five-year goal is to save the lives of over five million people and make a significant and lasting impact on the health-care industry."

"Wow," I replied, immediately understanding the power of the lesson Julian was presenting.

"You see, Peter, *the job of every leader is to define reality for his people.* He shows his people a better, brighter, more enlightened way to see the world. He takes the challenges they face and reframes them as opportunities for growth, improvement, and success. He does more than show people *how* to do things right — that is the job of the manager. The enlightened leader clarifies the right things to do, which gives his people compelling reasons to do what they do better than they have ever done it. He constantly reaffirms that the purpose everyone is striving toward is a good one and a just one and an honorable one. He understands that the best motivator for innovative and exceptional performance is meaningful work.

"And the truly visionary leader offers his followers hope by showing them that a higher reality exists for them if they keep moving in the direction of the leader's vision. To put it another way, he instills a sense of passion within his people by engaging their hearts and minds through the power of his purpose. Napoleon Hill captured the sentiment when he said, 'Cherish your vision and your dreams as they are the children of your soul; the blueprints of your ultimate achievements,' while Orison Swett Marden wrote, 'There is no medicine like hope, no incentive so great, and no tonic so powerful as expectation for something better tomorrow.' Find a vision you can invest every ounce of yourself within, one that will become your driving force, your raison d'être, your life's work. The excitement and positive energy that you will generate will spill over into the entire organization."

"That makes so much sense, Julian. If I imagine a truly compelling cause or worthy vision for the future of GlobalView and effectively communicate it to my employees in a way that fulfills their hunger to contribute and makes a real difference, they *will* get excited about their work."

"Absolutely. Oh, and don't forget, stop being so focused on *what* you will get when you realize your vision, and begin to pay more attention to the *why* of what you are doing. By dedicating your energies to the worthy purpose lying behind what you are doing and taking the focus off the rewards, you will get to your destination far more quickly."

"Why's that?"

"I'll tell you a fable that Yogi Raman shared with me that will answer your question nicely. Once a young student traveled many miles to find a famous spiritual master. When he finally met this man, he told him that his main goal in life was to be the wisest man in the land. This is why he needed the best teacher. Seeing the young boy's enthusiasm, the master agreed to share his knowledge with him and took him under his wing. 'How long will it take before I find enlightenment?' the boy immediately asked. 'At least five years,' replied the master. 'That is too long,' said the boy. 'I cannot wait five years! What if I study twice as hard as the rest of your students?' 'Ten years,' came the response. 'Ten years! Well, then, how about if I studied day and night, with every ounce of my mental concentration? Then how long would it take for me to become the wise man that I've always dreamed of becoming?' 'Fifteen years,' replied the master. The boy grew very frustrated. 'How come every time I tell you I will work harder to reach my goal, you tell me it will take longer?' 'The answer is clear,' said the teacher. 'With one eye focused on the reward, there is only one eye left to focus on your purpose.'"

"I won't forget that one, Julian."

"It's full of truth, isn't it? Rather than focusing on what he could give by reaching his ultimate destination, the boy's mind was centered on what he would receive. And therefore, it would take him far longer to get there. What I'm really trying to say, Peter, is that *you need to concentrate on contribution. Giving begins the receiving process*, that's the irony. By rallying around a worthy cause and constantly asking, 'How can we serve?' the rewards flow in degrees you cannot imagine. As they say in the East, 'A little bit of fragrance always clings to the hand that gives you roses.' "

"So true, when one really thinks about it," I admitted.

"Here's a great example. Southwest Airlines has consistently been one of the most successful major airlines. Herb Kelleher, its feisty and innovative leader, could easily have defined the purpose of the company in terms of 'being a great airline' or in terms of levels of profit or in terms of customer satisfaction. But he didn't. He had the wisdom to understand that by rallying his people around an emotionally compelling cause, Southwest would become a great airline, make huge profits, and generate an army of satisfied customers. So he defined his company's work — and its reality — in a way that truly connected with people."

"How did he do that?"

"He explained that Southwest was a very special airline run by very special people. He showed his team how the low fares the company advertised allowed people who could previously never afford air travel the opportunity to fly on a regular basis. This meant that grandparents could start visiting their grandchildren more frequently and that small-business people could explore markets they never could have before. He showed his people how their work was really about helping others fulfill their dreams and live better lives. He understood that *one of the key tasks of the visionary leader is to engage hearts.*

"And once he did, everything else he hoped for followed. So find a way for you and your managers to show your people that their work, directly or indirectly, touches people's lives. Show them that they are needed and important, and satisfy their hunger to make a difference. This is what the First Ritual of Visionary Leaders is all about. *Because when you link paycheck to purpose, you connect people to a cause higher than themselves. Your people will start to feel good about what they are doing. And when your people feel good about the work they do, they will begin to feel good about themselves as people. That's when real breakthroughs start to happen.* As Henry Ford once said, 'No one is apathetic except those in pursuit of someone else's objectives.' Give your people a slice of ownership in your vision. They will reward you with the gift of fidelity to your leadership."

"Come to think of it," I interjected, "recently I heard of a similar example of connecting to a compelling cause. During World War II, the workers who made parachutes for the Allied Forces were less than enthusiastic about their jobs, which could be described as tedious at best. They spent their days doing the same things over and over again and eventually grew weary of their work. Then one day, one of the leaders of their organization sat them all down and reminded them of the value of their work. He told them that it just might save the lives of their own fathers, sons, brothers, and compatriots. He reminded them that their work saved lives. By reconnecting them to the big picture, he made productivity go through the roof."

Julian then reached over to pick up a newspaper someone had left on the table next to us, which he thrust in front of me. As I squinted to see the picture on the front page in the dim porch light, Julian remarked, "I read the paper earlier today and came up with an insight I'd like to share with you. What do you see right here on this page?"

"Looks like a photo of the earth, like the ones the space-shuttle astronauts have been taking."

"Right. This afternoon, under the midday sun, I looked at that newspaper photo with my magnifying glass. Guess what I saw?"

"No idea."

"I saw that it was actually made up of nothing more than thousands of tiny black dots. Try it yourself tomorrow morning over a cup of coffee. You'll see that every single picture in the entire paper is nothing more than a collection of ink dots."

"Okay, so what's your point, Julian?"

"My point is that when you ask someone what the subject matter of this photograph is, he or she will quickly tell you that it is of the earth. No one will ever tell you he or she sees ten thousand dots clumped together. When viewing the pictures in the newspaper, we have trained ourselves to focus on the big picture, to observe the subject matter from a higher perspective. Yet, too often in business, leaders and managers lose all perspective and spend their days focusing on the little things."

"On the dots," I interjected, grasping the power of Julian's excellent analogy.

"You got it. And in doing so, they miss a world of opportunities, just like anyone focusing on the dots that make up this picture would miss this spectacular view of our world. To be a visionary leader, you must stay focused on the big picture — the compelling cause that lies at the heart of your vision. You must keep your people centered on the communities they are helping and on the lives they are touching. That will provide all the motivation they need."

"But doesn't it take a special kind of person to want to work hard for his or her company because it is doing good work and advancing 'an emotionally compelling cause,' to use your words? I'll be honest, all my people care about is getting their paychecks. They couldn't care less about the company or the vision it has."

"That's your fault."

"What do you mean?"

"Stop blaming your people for your leadership failures. Stop blaming the changing economy, increased regulation, and competitive pressures. If people haven't bought in to your vision, it's because they haven't bought in to your leadership. If they are not loyal, it's because you have not given them enough reasons to be loyal. If they are not passionate about their work, it's because you have failed to give them something to be passionate about. Assume total responsibility, Peter. Understand that *great leadership precedes great followership.*"

The truth of what Julian had just said rocked me. None of the management seminars I'd attended or consultants I'd worked with had ever offered me this kind of insight. And yet I knew it was right. Something inside me, intuition perhaps, confirmed that this youthful and vibrant-looking man in the robes of a monk was sharing the kind of wisdom that would profoundly affect my leadership and even my life. I knew I lacked a clear vision for the future and that all those around me could sense this failure. I knew my sense of uncertainty about the future was being telegraphed throughout the company by my temper tantrums and lack of confidence. And I knew my people did not respect or trust me. Julian was absolutely right. They had not bought in to my leadership.

"Great followership begins the day your people sense you truly have their best interests in mind," Julian continued. "Only when they know you care about them as people will they go to the wall for you. When you start putting your people before your profits, you will have accomplished something even more powerful than engaging their hearts. You will have earned their trust. Never forget that the real secret to being seen as trustworthy is to be worthy of trust."

It was now 10:00 P.M., and Julian and I were the only two people remaining on the golf club's veranda. I thought of suggesting to my friend that we move our conversation over to my home, but then decided against it. The night was nothing short of perfect. The sky was strikingly clear and glittered with a thousand stars. A full moon illuminated the area where we sat and lent a mystical feeling to what had already been a most unusual day. Julian was deeply engrossed in our conversation, and the leadership wisdom was flowing out of him with eloquence and grace. I would be a fool to do anything else but listen intently to this man who had learned so much during his time high in the Himalayas. I owed this at least to the people in my company.

"Mind if I ask you another basic question, Julian?"

"Not at all. That's why I'm here," he replied.

"How do visionary leaders show their followers that they really do have their best interests in mind?"

"Excellent question, Peter. The first thing to do is to practice the Principle of Alignment."

"Never heard of it."

"The Principle of Alignment holds that when your emotionally compelling cause, what we have simply called your 'vision,' is aligned with the interests of the people under your leadership, you will generate enormous levels of trust, loyalty, and commitment. Make sure your future vision is shared by all those you lead. *Too many vision statements hang on office walls rather than live in human hearts.* Give your people, from your top managers to your frontline workers, a genuine sense of ownership in the cause your organization is moving toward. A *shared* vision lies at the heart of every world-class organization."

"And how do I accomplish this?"

"You must show them that by helping you achieve your future goals they will also realize *their* future goals. By integrating what is meaningful to you with what is meaningful to them or, at the very least, by showing them how the attainment of the vision you hold for the company will help them feel fulfilled, they will come to understand that you care about their hopes and dreams. They will come to trust you. And with trust dominating the corporate culture, achievements once viewed as impossible become probable."

Julian added: "There is a second way to gain the respect and loyalty of the men and women you have the privilege to lead. And that is to become a liberator."

I had no idea what he meant, but, not wanting to ask too many silly questions, I simply nodded.

"You have no idea what I'm talking about, do you, Peter?" Julian observed.

"No, not really," I admitted, feeling like a school kid might after being caught in a tiny lie.

"Then why did you nod?" he demanded. "I don't mean to come across as being harsh because that's not what I'm about. I'm here this evening as a friend as well as a teacher who will give you the knowledge you need to fix your dying company and repair your leadership. But be honest. Honesty is one of the most important leadership skills. Remember, truth precedes trust. And people can sense sincerity a mile away. Without it, GlobalView will never grow to greatness."

"Okay, I'm sorry. I just didn't want to look foolish."

"Visionary leaders care more about doing what's right than appearing intelligent. Never forget that. Leadership is not about popularity, it's about integrity. It's not about power, it's about purpose. And it's not about title but rather talent. Which brings me squarely back to the point I was trying to make."

"I'm all ears," I offered sincerely.

"Visionary leaders see themselves as liberators rather than limiters of human talent. Their primary priority is to develop their people's full potential. They realize that every leader's task is to transform the workplace into a place of realized genius. The visionary leader understands that his company must, above all else, become a place and opportunity for self-development and personal fulfillment. He has the wisdom to know that in order for his followers to become deeply committed to his vision and offer the true extent of their capacities, he is duty-bound to provide them with challenging work. He must offer them a chance to grow as people through their work. You see, Peter, Yogi Raman told me that another of the human hungers is the need for growth and self-actualization. And visionary leaders satisfy this hunger by freeing people's strengths.

"Every single person on this planet has a deeply felt desire to expand and improve as a person. When you, as a leader, dedicate yourself to liberating rather than stifling the talents of the people under your leadership, you will reap quantum results in terms of loyalty, productivity, creativity, and devotion to your compelling cause. The bottom line is simply this: *people who feel superb about themselves generate superb results.* This leadership truth has stood the test of time. Never neglect it.

"The sad fact is that most people have no idea how much talent and potential slumbers within them. William James, the founder of modern psychology, once said, 'Most people live — whether physically, intellectually or morally — in a very restricted circle of their potential being. We all have reservoirs of life to draw upon, of which we do not dream.' And he was right. If the average person caught even a glimpse of how powerful he or she truly is, that individual would be astonished. And yet most people have never taken the time to look within themselves to discover who they really are."

"Did the sages teach you that principle?"

"Yes, they did. As a matter of fact, Yogi Raman loved telling me a story on that very point. According to Indian mythology, all people on earth were once gods. However, they began to abuse their power, so the supreme god, Brahma, decided he would take this gift away from them and hide the godhead in a place where they would never find it. One advisor suggested it be buried deep within the ground, but Brahma didn't like that idea. 'Mankind will one day dig deep enough to find it,' he said. Another advisor suggested it be hidden in the deepest part of the ocean. 'No,' said Brahma, 'one day mankind will dive deep enough to discover it.' Yet another advisor suggested the godhead be placed on the highest peak of the highest mountain, but Brahma replied, 'No, mankind will eventually find a way to climb to the top and take it.' After silently thinking about it, the supreme god finally found the ideal resting place for that greatest of all gifts. 'Here's the answer: Let's hide it within man himself. He will never think to look there.'"

"Great story," I offered sincerely.

"What I'm really trying to tell you, Peter, is that all people have more energy and ability within them than they could ever imagine. Your job, as a leader, is to uncover this truth for the benefit of your people."

"I hear what you are saying, Julian. But do you really believe that *everyone* has the potential for genius within them?"

"Genius is all about having an exceptional natural ability. We all have our special gifts and capacities. The problem is that most leaders have never offered their people opportunities to test and liberate those gifts. Rather than showing them what success looks like and then letting them use their creativity and resourcefulness to get there, the vast majority of leaders micromanage and dictate the path to be followed at every step of the way. They treat their team members as children, as if they are absolutely incapable of independent thought. Over time, this type of leadership stifles imagination, energy, and spirit. Then the leaders cry about a lack of innovation, productivity, and performance. 'Leaders should lead as far as they can and then vanish,' wrote H. G. Wells. 'Their ashes should not choke the fire they have lit.'

"So allow your people to flourish as they work toward your shared vision. Show them the truth about their talents and offer them blinding glimpses of a new world of opportunity. Challenge them and allow them to grow. Let them try new things and learn new skills. Let them fail from time to time, since failure is nothing more than learning how to win — free market research if you will. *Failure is the highway to success.* Understand that the visionary leader has the wisdom to push his people up rather than keep them down. He understands that when his people succeed, he succeeds. He understands exactly what Bernard Gimbel meant when he stated: 'Two things are bad for the heart — running uphill and running down people.' "

Julian's face was now fully animated, and his hands were gesturing in his passion for what he was saying. "Yogi Raman put it far more eloquently than I ever could," Julian continued. "Late one night, high in the mountains under a magnificent sky, he used a phrase that will always stay with me. It speaks volumes about the essence of visionary leadership."

"What was the phrase?" I asked impatiently.

"He told me that *'the ultimate task of the visionary leader is to dignify and honor the lives of those he leads by allowing them to manifest their highest potential through the work they do.'* "

"Powerful statement," I said softly, looking up at the sky in an effort to let the words soak in.

"And it's true. 'In dreams begin responsibilities,' proclaimed the poet Yeats. The visionary leader owes his people the responsibility of helping them develop and flourish. He understands that *the greatest privilege of leadership is the chance to elevate lives.* You need to keep uncovering the truth about their potential so they can see what they really are and what they truly can achieve. The great psychologist Abraham Maslow said that 'the unhappiness, unease, and unrest in the world today are caused by people living far below their capacity,' and I know he was right."

"Okay, here's another question. If the visionary leader's primary duty is to bring out the best in his people and bottom-line concerns are not important, how does he measure success?"

"I didn't say that the visionary leader disregards the bottom line, Peter. Of course he understands that for his company to grow, profits must flow. Productivity issues, customer satisfaction, and quality are all essential issues that occupy his attention. But first and foremost are the development and enrichment of his people. He actually sees his people as bundles of human potential just waiting to be unleashed for a worthy purpose. And he knows that when people work and live at their highest levels, the profits are certain to come. So to answer your question, the visionary leader measures his success through how many lives he touches and how many people he transforms. He measures his success, not by the extent of his power, but by the number of people he empowers. Makes sense?"

"It does, Julian. It really does. Okay, what comes next?"

"Then once you and your managers have begun to liberate the highest potential of your people, keep clarifying and communicating your great vision for the future. Productivity and passion are the inevitable by-product of men and women working toward an emotionally compelling cause. Inspire them to invest their energies and spirits in it. Allow them to feel it's theirs, and understand the implications of its achievement. Nothing focuses the mind better than a future ideal that moves the heart. Abe Lincoln knew this, Gandhi knew this, Mandela knew this, and so did Mother Teresa."

"I'll be totally honest. I still don't have a clear future vision of what you call 'an emotionally compelling cause' that I can get my team to rally around. I really liked your earlier example about saving the lives of five million people. I got excited about that idea, and I'm sure my people could as well. I guess that's a great starting point. Do you have any advice about how a leader can actually develop his or her vision for the future?"

"I don't mean to be trite, Peter, but it does take a lot of work.

You need to spend days and weeks reflecting on what things are most meaningful to you and where GlobalView can make the greatest contribution and impact. Take the time to be silent and begin to cultivate the power of your imagination. Envision what you want this organization to look like five, ten, and fifteen years from now. Awareness precedes change, so become aware of all the possibilities the future presents.

"Another tactic you can use to define your future vision is to analyze what keeps you up at night. What things are disturbing you and your customers. Go beyond simply satisfying their needs. Every good company does that. Strive to remove the *frustrations* from their lives. That's the real secret to having a loyal core of satisfied customers. Begin to anticipate what things bother them and define your future vision around these. And then here's the fundamental thing you need to do: once you have a clear focus for the future, constantly check it against the present state of operations. If your vision is an inspiring one, you will notice there is a gap. From this gap between where you now are and where you are going will emerge your strategy for change. Then exert your leadership influence to ensure that your blueprint for the future soon becomes the company's reality. Remember, 90 percent of success lies in the implementation and execution. *One of the hallmarks of visionary leadership lies in the translation of positive intentions into tangible results.*"

"So visionary leaders are people of action. They constantly push themselves to find better and faster ways to merge the present with the future and realize their vision. Is that accurate?"

"Yes, it is. They understand the ancient Law of Diminishing Intent and make sure it doesn't apply to them."

"I've never heard of that one."

"The Law of Diminishing Intent says that the longer you wait to implement a new idea or strategy, the less enthusiasm you will have for it. I think anyone who has worked in the corporate world knows the feeling of rushing out of a motivational seminar full of great ideas that will change every aspect of his or her life. But then the demands of the day compete for our attention, and all our good intentions and personal promises for change get pushed to the wayside. And the longer we put them off, the lower the probability we will ever fulfill them. So the lesson is to act daily on your strategy for change before it dies a quick death, burying your future vision with it. As the German philosopher Johann von Goethe said many years ago: 'Whatever you can do and dream you can do, begin it. Boldness has genius, power, and magic.' "

"So simple and yet so profound, Julian," I responded, trying to fully absorb these words of wisdom.

In the few hours I'd been with Julian this evening, I'd learned more about the craft of leadership than I had in all my previous years in business. Much of it really was common sense, but then, as Voltaire observed: "Common sense is anything but common." I guess I'd just never taken the time to think deeply about the elements of leadership and how I could implement them in our company. My days were filled with so many seemingly immediate brush fires to tend to that I was neglecting the fundamentals of effective leadership.

Ironically, due to this neglect, things were going from bad to worse. It made me think about the story of the lighthouse-keeper that my grandfather used to tell me. The lighthouse-keeper had only a limited amount of oil to keep his beacon lit so that passing ships could avoid the rocky shore. One night, the elderly man who lived close by needed to borrow some oil to light his home, so the lighthouse-keeper gave him some. Another night, a traveler begged for some oil to light his lamp so he could continue his jour ney. The lighthouse-keeper also complied with this request and gave him the oil he needed. The next night, the lighthouse-keeper was awakened by a mother banging on his door. She prayed for some oil so that she could illuminate her home and feed her family. Again he agreed. Soon all his oil was gone and his beacon went out. Many ships ran aground and many lives were lost because the lighthouse-keeper forgot to focus on his priority. He neglected his primary duty and paid a high price.

I realized I was heading down the same path as the lighthouse-keeper. I was not focusing on the timeless principles of enlightened, effective, and visionary leadership that Julian was sharing with me. Unless I simplified my leadership and stopped putting second things first, I sensed that I too would face disaster and be required to pay a particularly high price.

For the first time all night, Julian appeared weary. Many hours had passed since we had met on the veranda and Julian had startled me with his miraculous hole-in-one. Although he had clearly discovered many of the secrets of personal renewal along with the leadership truths he shared with me, he was still human after all and was entitled to be tired.

"Julian, I am so grateful to you for what you are doing. God knows, I need the coaching. You have spent the entire evening passionately teaching me some very powerful lessons that I know will lead to immediate improvements in my organization once I have the courage to implement them. I could listen to you all night. You always were a great speaker and dynamic conversationalist. But I want to be fair to you. Why don't we call it a night and meet first thing tomorrow morning in my office. I've kept the whole morning free in anticipation of our spending more time together. Let me drive you home now."

"Thanks for the offer, Peter. I must admit that I'm beginning to feel a little sleepy. I know that I look like a young man, but you know exactly how old I am. Though I feel more alive and vital now than I did when I was twenty, I still require a few hours of shut-eye to recharge the body and refresh the mind. If you don't mind, I think I'll walk back to where I'm staying. It's not too far from here anyway."

"But we're in the middle of the country, Julian. There's nothing but forest and farmland for miles," I offered, with real concern.

"Don't worry about me," Julian replied, clearly intending to keep his resting place a well-guarded secret. "I'll be just fine."

"So I'll see you tomorrow morning?"

"Actually, I'm busy tomorrow morning. And for the next few days, I have other matters I must attend to."

"You're not looking for a new Ferrari?" I joked, fully aware of the reply I would elicit.

"No, Peter. My Ferrari days are over. I've become a simple man bearing the simple truths that our world needs to hear. I promised Yogi Raman and the other sages that I would spend the rest of my life sharing their leadership wisdom with those who need to hear it. And that's exactly what I intend to do. How about if we meet next Friday? That will give you some time to contemplate what I've shared with you and put some of the philosophy into practice."

"Sure, Julian. If you want to meet next Friday, next Friday it will be. Same time, same place?"

"Actually, I'd like to meet you at a different location. Let's meet at that small park behind City Hall. There's something special there that I'd like you to see," he said, raising the suspense level. "C'mon, let me walk you down to your car. There's still a few quick leadership principles I'd like to leave you with."

We stood up and started walking toward the steps that would lead us down to the spot where I had parked my car. Suddenly Julian stopped.

"Do they still have that big-screen TV in the clubhouse?"

"Yes, they do. Why do you ask?"

"Just follow me. I need to demonstrate a point," he replied as he strolled across the darkened veranda and into the elegantly furnished clubhouse.

"Is this gentleman with you, Peter?" the manager asked me as we strode by, obviously uncomfortable with Julian's attire. I nodded and continued behind Julian, who had just stepped into the empty lounge where the big-screen television sat. Soon we were both sitting in front of it watching the evening news.

"Trying to catch up on the day's events?" I asked, unsure of my friend's intentions.

"Not really," came the reply as he pressed the button marked "radio" on the remote control he had picked up off the table in front of us. Now, the screen still showed the news, but the sound of the newscaster's voice was replaced by a soothing piece of classical music from one of the local radio stations. The contrast proved striking. Over the screen flashed pictures of the violence that plagues so many of our cities, and over the speakers came the serene strains of Vivaldi.

"Julian, what are you doing?"

"I'm sorry," he replied smiling knowingly. "Is there something wrong?"

"Of course there is. The video is not in synch with the audio."

"Just like too many leaders in our business world. They tell their customers they will do one thing and then do another. They preach fiscal restraint to their employees while they secretly negotiate their golden parachutes. They praise and show courtesy to a key executive when she is standing in front of them and then start condemning her the instant she leaves the room. They lack honor. They lack character. They lack integrity. *Their video is not in synch with their audio.*"

I had never thought about the power of integrity as a leadership philosophy. I was always of the "ends-justify-the-means" school of leadership and believed that sometimes one had to manipulate things to get the desired result. The more I reflected on it, the more I realized I had been acting as if the truth did not matter in our operations. Through my actions, I had been sending the message to others that little lies and deceits were okay. They were a normal and acceptable part of business. I would make up lame excuses as to why I could not meet with a manager facing a difficulty. I would break promises to key customers when the commitment interfered with a more pressing, and perhaps more rewarding, matter. Surely this influenced my people and the way they did business.

"Visionary leaders care less about appearing right than doing right," Julian added. "They don't see their leadership as a popularity contest where they need to please all their stakeholders. They have a very clear future focus, one that takes into account the interests of all, and they steadily move toward it. Their vision serves as their lighthouse, illuminating the path they must follow amid the turbulence that surrounds them. Their leadership is grounded by deeply rooted principles, principles that only add further fuel to their purpose and their inner fire. What they do is

aligned with what they say — they have character congruency. The leader with integrity will never let his lips betray his heart and will always let his principles guide his actions. Become a principled leader, Peter. Stand for something more than yourself. You will come to be respected. Maybe even revered."

"What kind of principles are you speaking of?"

"Collectively I call them the Gandhi Factor because they were the virtues that governed Mahatma Gandhi's life and leadership. They include honesty, industry, patience, perseverance, loyalty, courage, and perhaps, highest of all, humility. And, by studying them and building them into your leadership practices, you will transform the effectiveness of your entire company. When your leadership becomes moral as well as visionary, it will be as if GlobalView finally has an anchor to keep it from drifting when the seas get rough. When you face a crisis, there will be far less panic and far more calm. People will begin to act more fearlessly and more courteously and more respectfully. The nineteenth-century Spanish philosopher Carlos Reyles made the point splendidly when he wrote: 'Principles are to people what roots are to trees. Without roots, trees fall when they are thrashed with the winds. Without principles, people fall when they are shaken by the gales of existence.' "

"How do I bring the Gandhi Factor into our organization? I mean, things are pretty bad right now, and no one is open to anything new. Most of us feel that we've faced enough change over the past year alone to last us for many lifetimes."

"Be the model," came the simple reply. "I read awhile ago that Gandhi was once approached by a follower who asked the great man the secret to changing those around him. Gandhi thought for a moment and then replied, '*You* must be the change.' And that's really the secret to fostering character and integrity within

GlobalView. *You* need to be the change you desire. *Don't expect others to become anything more than you are willing to become yourself.* You need to be the model your followers will emulate. People do what people see. Seneca captured this point when he observed: 'I will govern my life and thoughts as if the whole world were to see the one and read the other.'

"What a quote. That's definitely one for the bulletin board in the lunchroom."

"Or the one in the executive suite," Julian replied firmly. "Visionary leaders become their own best ambassadors. They become shining examples of what they expect their people to be. Don't push your people to work harder with fewer resources while you take an extra afternoon off to play golf. Don't cut employee benefits while you, at the same time, refurbish your office. Don't tell your people to buy into your vision of the future while you quietly plan your exit strategy. People are not stupid. They can tell whether you are honorable or not. Live your leadership. Become one of those fine leaders who has the character power to go from knowing what's right to doing what's right to *being* what's right. Remember what Socrates said: 'The first key to greatness is to be in reality what we appear to be.'

My mind began to rifle through all the weaknesses my own character revealed on the job. I regularly said I'd do one thing and then did another. I generally cared more about my own interests than my people's. I had a fiery temper; I could be abrupt with my staff; I was self-centered, I was a very poor listener and often lacked sincerity. I thought no one really picked up on these flaws, but now I realized they did. For the first time in my entire executive career, I saw that my weaknesses as a leader were stimulating weaknesses in our company. My lack of leadership was the source of the lack of followership. It was time for me to stop blaming other people and other events for the difficulties GlobalView faced. It was time for me to clean up my act. It was time for me to "be the change."

"The imperfections of your character empower the imperfections of all those you lead," continued Julian. "When you are rude to an employee, you implicitly give him permission to be rude to someone else. When you lie to someone, you condone her lying to someone else. When you are late for a meeting, you silently say that punctuality is not important. And all these messages powerfully shape the corporate culture that serves as the framework for everything you and your followers do."

"How do I begin to be the model, Julian? I've practiced my current style of leadership for so long, I'm not sure where to start the change."

"First I suggest you do a Leadership Audit. Go deep within your heart and reflect on your strengths, and even more importantly on your weaknesses, as a leader. Get to know yourself. As I said earlier, *awareness precedes change.* Then, as with all change initiatives, whether personal or organizational, start off small. I recently read about a local company that was experiencing challenges similar to those of GlobalView. Morale was low, productivity had plummeted, creativity had dried up, and profits were nonexistent.

"The leader came up with a simple idea. Realizing that the fact that her frontline people rarely saw her was contributing to the company's poor performance, she began the simple discipline of taking regular walks around the shop floor. While doing so, she noticed that unlike her impeccable executive office upstairs, the factory was absolutely filthy. Garbage was strewn along the walkways, graffiti lined the walls and a thick coat of dirt clung to everything. Clearly, no one cared about the place where they worked.

"As the leader performed this regular walkabout, walking and talking with the workers, she would quietly pick up garbage, hoping that this symbolic gesture might somehow influence their thinking. Soon, the workers followed her example. While walking with her, they too would pick up the rubbish that had littered the floors and put it into the nearest trash can. Then, noticing how much better the place started to look, they asked the leader if they could paint the walls in the colors they wanted. She quickly agreed. Next came a wholesale clean-up effort, spearheaded by the factory workers, who now began to take great pride in their workplace. This, in turn, led to improved morale, improved productivity, and a sense of ownership in the minds of all of the employees. They had come to take a genuine interest in their work and in the organization they served. This positive force of change spread through the entire company, and it quickly returned to good health."

"And it all started with a simple act of the leader."

"Small acts can lead to great results, Peter. Never forget that your people are watching you. They are looking to you to see what is acceptable behavior and what isn't. So be the ideal of what you want your people to be. And borrow the strategy of that enlightened leader in the story. Get out of that palatial office suite you have barricaded yourself into and go talk to the people who really count — the men and women who look to you for leadership. Listen to them. Find out what makes them tick. Listen to their hopes and their dreams and their frustrations. Get a clear sense of what the environment is really like within your company. Most leaders haven't a clue. As Yogi Raman once told me, 'The fish is often the last to notice the water in which it swims.' "

With that sage advice, Julian shook my hand and began to head off into the darkness. Then he stopped and turned around. "Oh, there's something I forgot to give you. It will provide you with something to think about until we meet again next week." He reached into the long robe that he had refused to remove all evening, despite the intense heat. He pulled out an object I could not see due to the darkness and gently pressed it into my hand. Then he quickly disappeared into the night.

As I got into my car, I looked at Julian's gift under the small light next to the rearview mirror. It was another wooden piece of the jigsaw puzzle. Like the one before it, there was a design on it. And just as before, there were words carved into the wood. They read: *Ritual 2: Manage by Mind, Lead by Heart.*

The Ritual

Link Paycheck
to Purpose™

The Essence

The Ritual of a Compelling Future Focus

The Wisdom

- Purpose is the most powerful motivator in the world
- The primary task of the leader is to get his/her people excited about a compelling cause that contributes to the lives of others
- Great leadership precedes great followership. Show employees you have their best interests in mind.
- Visionary leaders focus on liberating human talent and manifesting the potential of people
- Lead with integrity, character, and courage

The Practices

- Ritualize wisdom so that your positive intentions translate into tangible results
- Communicate your compelling cause so it engages hearts
- Align your video with your audio

Quotable Quote

*The ultimate task of the visionary leader is to dignify
and honor the lives of the people he leads by allowing them to
manifest their highest potential through the work they do.*
The Monk Who Sold His Ferrari

RITUAL 2

❧

Manage by Mind,
Lead by Heart

CHAPTER SIX

The Ritual of Human Relations

It is the individual who is not interested in his
fellow men who has the greatest difficulties in life and
provides the greatest injury to others. It is from among
such individuals that all human failures spring.

Alfred Adler

As I DROVE HOME, my mind buzzed with the ideas Julian had
shared with me. They made so much sense that I wished I had
discovered them on my own, many years earlier. It would have
saved me so much aggravation and stress. If I had been applying
this leadership wisdom, who knows where GlobalView might be?
My mind then drifted off to what I wanted the company to look
like in ten years. I imagined what it would be like if we were the
biggest and best company in our field on the entire planet. I envi-
sioned how many of our people I could help develop and how many
people's lives we all could touch. A smile came to my face.

It felt good to be dreaming again. Jonas Salk once said,
"I've had dreams and I've had nightmares. I've overcome my

nightmares because of my dreams." All the successful business-people I had ever known had been dreamers. They had discovered their emotionally compelling cause through deep contemplation and had the courage to let it consume them. When we were hungry young entrepreneurs trying to build GlobalView, I would sit quietly for hours, doing nothing but thinking big thoughts about what our future might bring. But as the business grew, so did the headaches, and my quiet moments became scarce. This meeting with Julian, a man who had clearly experienced his own transfor-mation, would change me forever. I knew that I had the makings of a visionary leader. I just needed to learn what to do, and the leadership system Julian was sharing with me was showing me how. I felt great hope for the future, and the cloud of uncertainty began to lift. I felt inspired, renewed, and recharged.

That night, I ripped a sheet of paper off the legal pad that sat on the desk in my den. Although it was well past 2:00 A.M., I began to write down all that I had learned. I had been exposed to the First Ritual of Visionary Leaders: Link Paycheck to Purpose and the many timeless leadership truths that surrounded that great lesson. Julian had also given me a glimpse of the second of the eight rituals, a ritual that appeared to require me to Manage by Mind, Lead by Heart. And I knew there was still so much to come.

After committing what I had learned to paper, I began to list ways in which I could implement this knowledge. After all, Julian did warn me of what he called the Performance Gap, the theory that problems in leadership often arise when leaders fail to trans-late their good intentions into actions. Even from my own experi-ence in the business world, I knew that most ineffectiveness stems from the fact that most people do not have the self-discipline to do what they know they should do, when they have to do it. They put off doing the important things in business and in life in favor of the easy and immediate things. And then one day, late in their lives, these people wake up and realize what they could have done with their lives. They regret all the missed opportunities and lost chances. But, sadly, by then it's too late. It's like the saying: "If youth only knew. If age only could."

I thought deeply about my vision of GlobalView's future. I really went deep into my heart and asked myself where we could make the greatest impact as a company. I reflected on how I would start communicating to my people the vision that was taking form and how I would show them that by helping me fulfill my dream, they would fulfill theirs. I contemplated how my new vision for our future would make a difference in people's lives and how I could show my people that the work they did really mattered.

Then my mind began to focus on ways I could truly "be a liberator," to use Julian's words. To start seeing my role as a leader in terms of being a liberator and not a limiter of people's highest talents. I had to stop micromanaging and let people have more responsibility for their results. I had to start specifying goals and not methods so people could bring more creativity and ingenuity to their work. I had to let them develop as people on the job and challenge them more. I needed to let people do the jobs they were capable of doing, without my constant monitoring and supervision. And I had to bring back a sense of character and integrity to my leadership.

No more yelling and screaming. No more talking behind people's backs or keeping secrets. No more manipulating and arm-twisting. Sure, I had to be strong and tough when the circumstances required. That went without saying. But I also had "to stand for something," as Julian had said. I needed to govern myself and my leadership by the time-honored principles he had mentioned. The men and women of GlobalView deserved no less.

The days leading up to my next meeting with Julian whizzed by. I was so eager to meet him, I could hardly sleep at night. My energy level soared as the wisdom he had learned in the Himalayas became a part of my life. I cannot really explain why. I guess it was similar to the way parents feel when they have their first child. There is a newfound sense of excitement, passion, and purpose all mixed into one sentiment. You do not want to miss a moment of the experience and feel grateful that it has finally happened to you.

In the few days of applying the truths Julian had taught me, noticeable improvements began to take place within the company. I became more open, honest, and interested. I started to take the ideas and interests of others into account. I started to spread my sense of excitement around the company and communicate a much grander vision for the future of GlobalView. And I began to care about the people I worked alongside. Even my executive assistant, Arielle, a no-nonsense woman who rarely let down her guard around me, joked that I must have been replaced by "an alien clone from a kinder, wiser colony." "No matter what has happened, Mr. Franklin," she said in a slightly more serious tone, "everyone really likes the changes you are making and hopes that you will keep moving forward. And no one can believe the way you set fire to the old mission statement in the middle of the parking lot yesterday morning. It will go down in GlobalView history, that's for sure!"

Finally, Friday came. As I left our headquarters and drove down to the park behind City Hall where Julian had instructed me to meet him, my fingers toyed with the second piece of the puzzle Julian had given me. Ritual 2: Manage by Mind, Lead by Heart. *What exactly does that mean?* I wondered. So far Julian had offered me some great information. It was powerful yet practical. But this stuff about "leading by the heart" concerned me a little. I hoped Julian was not going soft on me.

Just as he had promised, Julian was waiting for me in the park. And although it was another scorching summer's day, he again wore the attire of the traditional monks whose ageless knowledge had changed his life. But in a strange twist, today he also wore a fashionable pair of dark sunglasses, the kind that rock stars and movie actors favored. The contrast was striking.

"I like the shades, Julian," I said as I patted him on the shoulder, glad to see my friend again.

"I thought you'd like them. I bought them from a young street vendor the other day. He told me I needed to update my look. So I did," he laughed. "I needed them anyway, to protect my eyes from that sun," he added, looking up into the sky for a second.

"Wouldn't want to lose your vision, right?" I replied, ever the model student.

"Nicely said, Peter. Sounds like you've been doing some thinking."

"True. Actually, I've taken your advice and have begun to do more than just think about the leadership wisdom you have given me — I've started to act on it."

"Wonderful! I knew I didn't make a mistake coming to see you. I knew you would put the priceless information the sages bestowed on me to good use. And as the sages themselves loved to say, 'When the student is ready, the teacher appears.'"

"And not a day too early, Julian. Things were getting insane at the company. Now I realize that. And yet, in just a few days of applying the lessons you've shared with me so far, I've noticed some very positive improvements," I said, pleased to inform him of our progress. "I know it's still early and real change takes time, but things are starting to happen. I've shared your leadership wisdom with everyone on my management team and every supervisor in the company. I've asked them to, in turn, pass along the lessons I've learned to every other person who works here so we can all grow wiser together. It's like you told me earlier: leadership is not really about position or title but about action. And anyone in the company, from my senior vice president of operations to the shop steward to the young kid who works in the mail room can display leadership. I now understand that every single employee at GlobalView must receive leadership training if we really want to be a world-class organization. Everyone must know what it means to be a visionary leader and then bring this knowledge to bear on the particular job that he or she does. Every one of us must strive to show leadership at work."

"Make sure you share your success stories with me as they come. I know there will be many," said Julian.

"Well, actually, I already have one I can mention. After our meeting at the golf club last week, I went home and wrote out a wish list of things I needed to change in my leadership. I did a Leadership Audit, as you suggested. I noted as many weaknesses as I could think of and then came up with an action strategy and a time line by which I would eliminate each one. Once I did that, I then had a little personal brainstorming session where I came up with hundreds of innovative ways I could implement the points you made when we last met. One of the ideas that came to me was to give all my employees a $1,000 annual budget that they could spend on enhancing their professional and personal effectiveness. You told me I had a duty to nurture the growth of my people on the job and to really help them get the best out of themselves. So I decided to take this duty seriously and really encourage personal development. You should have seen how happy they were when they heard about this initiative. I know it will cost a fair amount of money, but I really see it as an investment rather than as an expense. As you suggested, Julian, employees who feel superb about themselves are certain to produce superb results."

"So what have they started to do with the money?"

"Well, the program is just getting off the ground, but members of a few of our teams have already received their checks. From what I've heard, some of them are buying the planning tools they always felt they needed to effectively manage their schedules and their time. Others are spending their budgets on motivational books and educational audiocassette programs they can listen to in their cars on the way to work. And one man used part of his budget in a very private way. He is quite short and had difficulty performing his work in our manufacturing facility because it required him to continually reach up to high places. But he was too embarrassed to tell his supervisor. He thought everyone would laugh. Once he had his own budget to spend in any way that would enhance his on-the-job effectiveness, he went out and bought a simple footstool. His supervisor told me that his productivity has doubled and he has never seen the man happier."

"You are starting to experience the power of the truths I discovered in the Himalayas. The reason they have stood the test of time is pretty simple. Because they work."

"I'll tell you another thing I've started doing since you exposed me to your leadership wisdom, Julian."

"What's that?"

"I've started taking a lot more risks as a leader. I've begun to see myself as an innovator and catalyst for new ideas. If I'm not constantly stretching my mind and exploring new pathways of thought, how can I expect my people to do the same? I'm reading again. I'm making the time to think again. And I've even started taking a daily cruise around the office to get to know as many people as I can, like that leader you told me about. The fish is often the last to notice the water in which it swims, you know."

Julian smiled, clearly pleased at my progress, and said, "Risk taking is a very powerful success skill. Yet, most people have never cultivated this important leadership discipline. Most of us never remove our security blankets and venture into the zone of the unknown. Yogi Raman put it this way: 'The farther you go out on a limb, the easier it is to fall. But then again, out on the limb is where all the fruit is.' Visionary leaders take chances. They are constantly trying new things. And that becomes a habit. As Seneca said so many years ago: 'It is not because things are difficult that we do not dare; it is because we do not dare that they are difficult.'"

"I'll tell you another chance that I'm taking to clean the cobwebs out of our organization. I read about a top-performing company in Singapore that had a very unusual practice. Every other Friday afternoon, they would shut down the factory for two hours. Then, all the different teams would go off and discuss the latest management bestseller. It not only allowed them to cement relationships with their teammates and break out of their routines, it kept them abreast of the cutting-edge ideas on personal and organizational excellence."

"Tremendous concept," Julian replied as he sat down on the grass in a shaded spot.

"I've instituted the same practice at GlobalView. My managers are really excited about it. They've always complained they never have enough time to read the best business books and keep up with the current management trends. Now they'll be getting paid to do so," I noted proudly.

"Believe me," said Julian, "in the long run, this idea will save you money. The ineffectiveness that arises in most companies from outdated thinking and inefficient systems that continue to exist simply because of tradition is extremely costly over the long run. Even deadly. What you are doing might be unorthodox, but it is also smart. Putting your people first is the wisest leadership lesson you will ever learn. Which brings me to the next element of Yogi Raman's ancient system, the Second Ritual of Visionary Leaders: Manage by Mind, Lead by Heart."

"I was wondering what this one was all about."

"This is the ritual of human relations and communication competency. Every truly visionary leader has mastered the practice of connecting deeply to his followers. He has refined the art of clarifying his vision for the benefit of his people in a way that fully engages them and stirs them into action. Through their people skills and talents as effective communicators, such leaders touch the hearts of their team and earn long-term loyalty. Simply put, *When you enrich the relationship, you enhance the leadership.*"

"Are relationships really that important? I mean I know a ton of leaders who couldn't care less about connecting with their people. They see their missions very simply: to create profit and value for the shareholder. Everything else is irrelevant."

"These so-called leaders are not visionary leaders and, believe me, there is a big difference. Visionary leaders are not people who squeeze as much profit out of a company in as short a period as possible before they bail out and head for an early retirement in the Bahamas, leaving their company in a terrible mess. While short-term profits are important to visionary leaders, they are constantly thinking long-term. They understand that by taking the time to allow their people to develop the fullness of their potential and put strong systems in place, upon which the company can build, massive profits are guaranteed. The leaders you speak of are like sprinters running a marathon. They go for broke in the first mile, but in doing so have nothing left for the rest of the run. Ultimately, they are the biggest losers.

"You see, Peter, anyone can go into a company and drive up profits by relentlessly driving down his or her people. But soon, the people will grow tired and the equipment will break, because neither has been properly cared for. Remember, the chickens always come home to roost. You just can't avoid the natural laws of life."

"Point well taken, Julian. So what do I need to do to put Ritual 2 into practice?"

"I'm about to show you," he replied as he glanced at an elderly couple sitting under a nearby tree, giggling like a couple of school kids as they enjoyed their picnic. "See those two over there? I've been observing them for the past few weeks. Sometimes I've watched them feed the ducks in that pond over there. Sometimes I've watched them ride their bicycles around the park. Sometimes I've even overheard their conversations as I relaxed here on the grass," Julian admitted, with apparent embarrassment. "I'll tell you one thing for sure. Those two have a wonderful relationship."

"I wonder how long they've been married? They really look like they're in love."

"Forty-three years from what I've overheard," replied Julian. "Last week they celebrated their anniversary right here in this wonderful park. They shared a huge cake with a bunch of friends over there. Quite a lively party they had," he said, pointing over to a clearing dotted with five picnic tables and bright red flowers. "Forty-three years. That's pretty amazing in this day and age."

"It's not hard to see how they've managed to stay together so long," Julian said as he took off his sunglasses and wiped the perspiration from his face. "Not surprisingly, they follow the timeless human relations principles that Yogi Raman told me visionary leaders applied to foster the respect of their followers and to build lasting trust. And if there's one thing I've learned, a world-class organization is also a high-trust organization. Trust is one of the ageless elements of every peak-performing company. If your people don't trust you, their managers, and their co-workers, there is no way they are going to go the extra mile to give you their best efforts. Without trust, there is no commitment. And without commitment, there's no company."

"So what kinds of things have you observed this couple doing?" I asked with keen interest.

"Four things in particular, Peter: promise-keeping, aggressive listening, being consistently compassionate, and finally—and perhaps most important—truth-telling."

"Those are the secrets to their incredible relationship?"

"Yogi Raman taught me that those are the secrets to *every* great relationship. He told me that anyone who desires to be a visionary leader, one who inspires his or her people to achieve extraordinary things, must make these four practices an integral part of his or her leadership style. They are the cornerstones of effective human relations. They will help you perform Ritual 2 on a daily basis."

"They seem so simple. Can they really make the impact on my team that you are suggesting?"

"That's the problem with many of the enduring leadership truths. They appear to be so simple and so obvious that everyone puts off applying them. They are not trendy, so people shove them aside in favor of strategies that are more flashy and sensational. Let me ask you, Peter, are you doing these four things every day?"

"Uh, no."

"Let's deal with the first one at least. Do you keep the majority of the promises you make?"

I immediately knew the answer to this question. I would often break promises I had made. I would tell my employees I was always available to meet with them, but, when someone actually had a problem that he or she wished to discuss with me, I found convenient ways to get out of the meeting. Other times, I'd tell a key supervisor that she deserved to have the increased responsibilities she'd been asking for. But then I'd neglect to follow through and ensure she got what she wanted. I was a master of broken promises.

"Every promise you break, no matter how small and seemingly inconsequential, steadily chips away at your character," Julian said to break the silence. "Each time you don't return a phone call when you said you would or miss a meeting you promised to attend, you erode trust. Each time you don't honor a commitment, you chip away at the bonds between you and the people you have the privilege to lead. As Yogi Raman used to say, *'Every time you avoid doing right, you fuel the habit of doing wrong.'*"

"And those elderly lovebirds keep their promises to each other?" I wondered aloud.

"They sure do. When the husband says he'll meet his wife at noon for lunch over at that hot-dog stand, you can bet he'll be right on time. When the wife says that she'd like to take their bicycles out for a spin on a particular day, sure enough, their van pulls up into the parking lot and the husband wheels out the bikes. You see, Peter, when people keep their promises, they breed great loyalty. The wife knows she can count on her husband, and he knows he can count on her. And this breeds consistency, an important attribute of high-quality human relations. The husband and wife know what to expect of each other. They can rely upon each other. And that, in turn, breeds trust. Never get behind on your promises. I know you'll be delighted with the results."

"You know, Julian, you're the first person to show me the connection between promise-keeping and human relations. I know what you are saying is true. For me to really be the leader I've now committed myself to being, I must keep the promises I make to others and be a person they can truly count on. I need to earn the trust of my people and gain their loyalty. From today onward, I will be a man of my word. I'll do what I say I will do. I promise."

Julian grinned. "I'll hold you to that one, my friend."

The sun was still blazing as he stood up and started walking. It was remarkable how agile Julian was despite his advancing years. His youthful face carried a smile, as he strode around the park, continuing his discourse on Ritual 2 and the power of leading from the heart and enriching human relationships.

"The second discipline you must master to make Ritual 2 a part of your leadership style is aggressive listening. *Visionary leaders capture the hearts of their people by deeply listening to them.* Most leaders believe that to lead effectively, they need to do most of the talking. They have been brainwashed into believing that leaders speak and followers listen. Visionary leaders know that another of the human hungers is the hunger to feel understood. Everyone has a deep need to have a voice and to have that voice considered. So visionary leaders become excellent listeners. The irony is that in doing so, they become known as superb communicators."

"Let me get this right, Julian. Are you actually telling me that by listening more effectively, I'll be able to communicate my messages more effectively? I mean, how could that be possible?" I asked.

"You want your people to trust you, right?"

"Right."

"You want your people to be loyal to you and GlobalView, right?"

"Right."

"Then remember this: listening to what others have to say is a mark of respect. It shows you value your people and believe in them. What I'm really saying is that you must show empathy to them. You must identify with their perspectives. You must *invest yourself* in the person communicating with you. You need to truly get behind their eyeballs and discover what they are thinking. Only by doing so will you understand them and will they feel understood. And the person who feels understood is the person who listens when it's your turn to speak. Remember, Peter, one of the greatest gifts you can ever give anyone is giving them 100 percent of your attention. *Listening truly is the highest compliment.*"

"I've discovered that I'm not a great listener," I interrupted. "The more I think about it, the more I realize that my poor listening habits must really turn off the people I work with. By not paying attention to what they say and feel, I'm really telling them that I don't care, that what they say is not really important to me. It now seems so obvious. And I'll bet that's one of the root causes of our low morale and low-trust environment. I guess I just never thought that excellent listening skills were that big a deal."

"They are," Julian replied swiftly. "Let's see how poor they are. Let's do a quick audit."

"Must we?"

"Like I said before, Peter, awareness precedes change. Before you can improve your leadership skills, you must know precisely which skills need to be improved. *An unknown weakness can never be transformed into a strength.* So let me ask you, do you frequently interrupt others?"

"Guilty."

"Do you finish other people's sentences for them?"

"Once in a while," I lied.

"Are you rehearsing your response while the other person is speaking?"

"Maybe," I said defensively.

"Well, then, we both know you need to do some serious work in the listening department. If you truly want to master Ritual 2 and capture people's hearts, you must stop listening with the intent to respond. Instead, *listen with the intent to understand.*"

"Wow, that's a powerful way of expressing it, Julian. But let me ask you, if effective listening is such an important leadership discipline, why do so few of us do it?"

"Great question. The first reason is that human beings are visual creatures. Eighty-three percent of our sensory input comes through our eyes so we often neglect much of what we hear. Here's an example. You're invited to a cocktail party. You stroll in and are immediately introduced to someone. You begin chatting with that person and, after a few minutes, you realize you have forgotten something."

"To get a drink?" I quipped playfully.

"No, the person's name."

"Happens to me all the time."

"And not just to you. More than 90 percent of businesspeople forget the name of the person they've been introduced to eight seconds after they've heard it. The reason is that as soon as we meet someone new, our brains start processing all the visual and tactile information such as height, weight, gender, strength of handshake, and facial expression. In the process, the name escapes our attention.

"So we need to start paying more attention to what we hear," Julian continued. "The second reason most leaders are not excellent listeners is that human beings possess the ability to listen at a rate of about 500 words per minute, yet we speak at the much slower rate of 100 to 125 words per minute. With all that space left to fill, our minds tend to wander."

"Interesting. To be honest, I find that my mind constantly drifts off when I should be listening to others. I'll be in a meeting, and rather than listening to the speaker, my mind will rifle through all the urgent things that need to be done. Even when I'm talking to someone one on one, I start to daydream. Any ideas about how I can begin to focus on listening to and understanding the person speaking?"

"Excellent listening is a habit that takes a little time and practice. But believe me, it is worth the investment. I heard recently that listening can even improve your health by reducing your blood pressure, moderating your heartbeat, and making you feel calmer. Having said that, the goal is to become 'an aggressive listener,' to use the term that Yogi Raman coined. I know it sounds like a contradiction in terms, but it's not.

"Get excited about being a great listener; get passionate about understanding your people. As to how you do this, try these simple ideas. First, cultivate the skill of asking superb, open-ended questions of your employees and then really listen to the responses. One leader at a high-performing company came up with a simple yet effective idea to make the process even better. He recruited employees from throughout the organization and asked them for their detailed, practical suggestions about how to improve the company. This initiative had two immediate benefits. The first was that the employees felt they were being listened to, which further enhanced morale and environmental trust. The second benefit was that management received free advice about how to streamline and enhance the operation from the people who best knew its weaknesses rather than from an expensive outside consultant. Management then took the best suggestions and scientifically tested them against solid performance measures such as sales revenue, customer service complaints, and quality standards to see which ones actually worked. By listening to its people, that company became a market leader."

"Okay, I'm with you on this one," I replied. "Can you tell me more about these 'open-ended' questions you mentioned?"

"An open-ended question such as, 'What things can I do to help you do your job better' will elicit a very different response than a closed question such as, 'If I bought you a new computer, it would help you, wouldn't it?' Then develop a series of what I call 'head-snappers.' These are powerful questions designed to get your people to open up and connect with you."

"Any examples?"

"'What has been your greatest achievement on the job?' 'What are you happiest doing?' 'What three things could we do to make this company more successful?' 'What excites or motivates you?' and 'What would you do if you were leading this company?' are all good ones. But I suggest that you take some time to come up with your own. My point is that you must become good at asking questions. And just in case you think I'm telling you to become a wallflower, never forget that the person asking the questions is actually leading the conversation."

"Really?"

"Really. The second strategy I suggest you apply to develop more aggressive listening skills is to briefly summarize and paraphrase what you have heard. By doing so, you will ensure that you have understood the other person's message and that she feels understood."

"Exactly how do I summarize and paraphrase?"

"Develop expressions such as, 'Just to make sure I understand you properly, are you saying . . . ?' Believe me, Peter, questions like that will work magic in terms of human relations and your competency as a communicator. Another powerful strategy is to take notes. Imagine what your people will think when they see you pull out a pad of paper and a pen and jot down notes as they speak. This simple gesture will send them the message that you are serious about taking them seriously. And then finally, be sincere. The suggestions I've offered you are not tricks and tactics designed to manipulate people. They are aids to help you connect with your followers. But if you are not genuinely concerned, they will sense it and the trust and respect you seek will never flow."

"And I suppose that couple over there listens to each other?"

"Most definitely. When the wife speaks, the husband is engaged and attentive. When the husband speaks, the wife summarizes and paraphrases to show him she identifies with what he is saying. I'm not suggesting that I spend my days listening to the private conversations of these two fine people, but I've heard enough to know they have mastered the art of excellent listening. And so should you."

"Okay. I'm sold on the concept. Like all the other leadership wisdom you've shared with me, it makes so much sense. Just to make sure I understand you properly, are you saying that I should practice Ritual 2, leading from the heart, by keeping my promises and becoming an aggressive listener?"

Julian beamed, knowing that I had just put his "summarize and paraphrase" strategy into play. Then he patted me on the back and said, "C'mon, let's get a hot dog."

"You still eat hot dogs?" I asked in surprise. After all, Julian had attributed much of his physical transformation to the healthful diet the sages had taught him while he was living in the Himalayas.

"It's for you, my friend. You must be hungry, " he said with concern.

As we continued to walk, Julian revealed another of the timeless truths about human relations that he promised would foster greater respect, loyalty, and commitment.

"Visionary leaders are consistently compassionate. They constantly show kindness to their team and think about ways to show their concern is sincere. You see, Peter, another of the human hungers is the need to be cherished. To quote the eminent Harvard psychologist, William James: 'The deepest principle of human nature is the craving to be appreciated.' It doesn't matter

who you are — whether you are a young schoolgirl or the toughest factory worker — every single person on this planet has a burning desire to be treated well. The best leaders know this and fulfill that need by being consistently compassionate."

"What exactly does being 'consistently compassionate' involve?"

"It's all about letting your humanity shine at work. It's about showing people courtesy, consideration, and respect, every single day of the work week. And courtesy is incredibly important in business. Peter Drucker once noted that manners are the lubricant of an organization. So be kind to the people you lead. Respect and cherish them. I think Goethe captured it perfectly when he said: 'Treat people as if they were what they ought to be and help them become what they are capable of being.' That, my friend, is one of the great secrets of leadership success."

"But, if you don't mind me saying, Julian, if I were constantly kind to my people, wouldn't I look soft? I've always heard the best leaders are the tough ones."

Julian was silent as he bought me a thick hot dog and then watched me slather mustard and relish over it. I sensed he knew my question was important and wanted to gather his thoughts.

"Visionary leaders blend humanity with courage," came the poetic reply. "All too often, leaders are not real."

"What do you mean?" I asked as I munched on my lunch.

"Many leaders share the belief you just expressed. They have been told that effective leaders are tough, autocratic leaders. They feel that being nice isn't part of their job description and that leaders shouldn't appear too kind. And, therefore, even though the majority are decent people, they hide their true selves and always act tough, sending waves of fear through their organizations. The sad thing is that a dictatorial style of leadership inevitably leads to only two outcomes: people become afraid or they begin to rebel. Either way, the company is soon surpassed by its competitors. Florence Nightingale hit the nail on the head when she mused: 'How very little can be done under the spirit of fear.' "

Julian paused and then added, "I'm not saying that visionary leaders are not strong. They are tough when the circumstances call for it. Actually, they are the strongest of all leaders because it requires great courage to maintain fidelity to one's vision and constantly do what's right. But they never neglect their people's interests. No matter how busy they get, they always take the time to show they care. They don't mind showing they are human. And that vulnerability powerfully connects them to their followers and builds lasting bonds.

"What I'm asking you to do, Peter, if you truly are committed to making GlobalView a world-class operation, is to forget about all those clever new management fads that are popping up in business journals and focus on the timeless truths of leadership. One of the greatest of these is that what people really want is a leader who values and cherishes them as people. They want a leader who has the vision to give them a glimpse of a compelling cause they can strive toward so that their daily work becomes meaningful. Above all, they seek a leader who is kind."

"So how do I go about being 'consistently compassionate'?"

"Just look at those two lovebirds," came the reply, as Julian pointed to the elderly couple, just as the husband had reached into the picnic basket and pulled out a large straw hat to protect his bride from the hot sun. "That man constantly performs what Yogi Raman called '*minor acts of caring.*' He always looks for ways to show his wife he is concerned for her welfare. Sometimes he offers her shade by holding up an umbrella. Other times he pours her a cold drink from the canteen. A couple of weeks ago, when it started to rain heavily, I actually saw him lift her over a large puddle in an effort to keep her dry."

"What are you suggesting, Julian? You can't be telling me that I should be getting cold drinks for my people or lifting them up over the puddles that regularly flood our parking lot?" I remarked, tongue in cheek.

"Of course not. You know me better than that. Even when I was that hard-driving, fast-living lawyer, I always had my feet firmly planted in the real world. What I'm saying is look for ways to spread 'minor acts of caring' through your entire organization. Like I said earlier, be the model. The leader teaches his followers what behavior is acceptable by his or her own behavior. Look for small ways to show you care."

"Such as?"

"Such as sending a handwritten thank-you card to an employee who has done a great job. One CEO I knew personally signed a Christmas card to every one of his 10,000 employees. He would start in January in order to be sure he would get them all done in time for the following December, writing a few each day. Sure it took a few minutes from his busy schedule. But you can't tell me it didn't make an impact on his people. Or perhaps you might start answering your own phone — as Sam Walton did. Why not stroll down the hallways and talk to your people, being truly interested when you ask, 'How's the family?' Paul Allaire, as the head of Xerox, would have a photographer photograph him with one of his top producers and then offer the portrait to the salesperson as a keepsake for a job well done. These small acts of kindness make a profound statement. They add up over time and show your people you are committed to them. They show you care. Give more of yourself to those you lead. Albert Einstein said wisely: 'Many times I realize how much of my own outer and inner life is built upon the labors of my fellow men and how earnestly I must exert myself in order to give in return as much as I have received.' "

"I agree, Julian. Sure I'm busy, but I know I could do at least a few of these things to make a deeper connection with the men and women of my organization. You are saying that small actions can have big consequences, right?"

"Exactly. In 1963, meteorologist Edward Lorenz postulated a simple theory: the flapping of a butterfly's wings in Singapore could affect a hurricane in North Carolina. To the amazement of everyone in the meteorological community, Lorenz showed that it could, turning upside down the long-held view that the universe was a large machine in which causes matched effects. Lorenz's postulation became known as the Butterfly Effect and stands as a reminder of the natural principle that small actions can have big consequences. Minor acts of caring are no different, Peter. A personal phone call when one of your employees becomes a new parent or a quick visit with a worker who is facing a challenge makes a world of difference in terms of the way people see you. Remember, you can't fax a handshake."

"You mentioned a fourth discipline I could use to ensure that I practice Ritual 2 and truly lead from the heart. What was it?"

"After keeping your promises, listening aggressively, and being consistently compassionate, the final cornerstone of human relations and communications competency is truth-telling. The best leaders, those who win the hearts and minds of those they lead, are open and honest. Actually, they are *fanatically honest* and, by being so, they earn everyone's trust. They also share information with everyone and make it one of their highest priorities to keep their people informed. They know that the long-term success of their leadership depends upon their information sharing and truth-telling in all circumstances."

"And what do you mean when you say the best leaders are 'open'?"

"To truly win people's support and deep commitment to your future vision, you must communicate as much key information as possible to them. The more they know about what you are doing, the more they'll invest in where you are going. Just as with aggressive listening, being open and sharing ideas with people is a mark of respect. Having the decency to quickly and accurately inform them of the things that will affect them shows them that they are important. It shows them you value them. And when you constantly keep the lines of communication open, your employees will begin to value you as a leader, so much so that they will not want to let you down. That's when the magic starts."

"What do you mean?"

"Yogi Raman believed the highest level a visionary leader can attain in terms of the quality of the relationship she has with her people comes when they believe so deeply in her leadership that they will do almost anything not to let her down. And when that happens, all things become possible within that organization."

I knew I fell far short of the model leadership Julian spoke of. I belonged to the school that believed the less employees knew about what was going on within the company the better. Anything other than the information they needed to do their specific jobs was none of their business. But what Julian said was true. People who were fully informed would soon understand the rationale for my decisions. They would have greater confidence in my leadership because they would know the context from which I was acting. And they would certainly feel a greater sense of ownership in the company. What Julian was telling me was not just the right thing to do. It was the smart thing to do.

"Being open and truthful also means that you take care of the little issues and skirmishes that come up every day before they escalate into full-blown wars," Julian added.

"You've lost me again."

"Here's an example. One well-known company suffered from major problems in morale when a key executive was let go. Rumors that the former executive's division was in trouble began to run rampant and other employees began to fear they would lose their own jobs. Fortunately, the company's president was a visionary leader. Because he understood the importance of openness and honesty, he immediately called a meeting to explain exactly what had happened. The executive had only been hired on a short-term basis to improve the productivity and effectiveness of the division he was charged to lead. Since the executive fulfilled his mandate and the division was again performing well, the president decided that there was simply no need to renew his contract. Although disappointed, the executive knew from the outset that this was a short-term post and left on good terms. By being totally candid with his people and keeping them in the loop, the president actually turned a negative into a positive."

"How so?"

"Because he helped them to see the executive's departure in a better light. He made them realize that it was actually a reason to celebrate because it meant that a division that had once performed poorly was now in fine shape, running smoothly without the benefit of an outside turnaround specialist. By being open with his people, the president showed them a more positive reality and nipped the problem in the bud. Don't let issues build. Explain the reasons behind your decisions and be transparent with your people. That's what leadership is all about, my friend. As I said before, you need to help define reality for your people, and keeping them informed will greatly assist you in doing that. Problems won't grow and misunderstandings won't fester. Now, if you don't mind, I must leave you. There's something I must do. It's been a great day. Thanks for being such a good student."

"Where are you rushing off to?" I asked.

"I'm going to watch the stars," came the mysterious reply.

"What do you mean?"

"I'll tell you about it later, when you're ready for it. I've got to run."

What was it about Julian and the stars? During our meeting at the golf club, I remember him looking up at one of the stars and muttering a few words to himself. Now he was dashing off to do more of the same thing. Frankly, it sounded a little flaky, especially for Julian. After all, in his previous incarnation, this guy had been a corporate superstar. He had graduated at the top of his class at Harvard Law School and had been one of the finest lawyers in the entire country. Now he was running around in monk's robes and stargazing. I never could figure Julian out. I guess that was part of his charm.

"But wait, Julian," I replied anxiously. "Don't I get another piece of the puzzle? And when can we meet again? You can't leave me hanging like this. I really want to master the whole of Yogi Raman's leadership formula. It's already working its miracles within GlobalView."

"Here, take this," he said, handing me a ticket for a court side seat at the next home game of the Skyjumpers, our local professional basketball team.

"I don't get it, Julian. What's this for?"

"We'll meet at the game. There's something very special I need to show you there. And it'll give me a chance to buy you another hot dog. You inhaled the one I bought you for lunch. Lucky I didn't lose a finger!" he quipped.

With that, he was gone. I started walking back to my car, which I had left at the other end of the park. Julian had offered me so many ideas to improve my company that I tingled with excitement. I couldn't wait to put Ritual 2 and all its components into practice. I felt hopeful for the future and deeply grateful that this sage man had returned to share his knowledge with me. As I drew closer to my car, I saw something tucked under the windshield wiper.

Oh no, not another parking ticket. I've already had three this week, I thought to myself.

But I soon realized it was not a ticket. Rather, it was an envelope with the letters "J.M." elegantly embossed upon it. This was Julian's personal stationery from the old days. I grabbed it from under the wiper and peeked inside, unsure what surprise it held. I wasn't disappointed.

It was the third piece of the jigsaw puzzle that I had been hoping for. Like the others, this wooden piece had some words carved on it. I now knew they would offer me a clue to the third ritual of the ancient leadership system Julian had discovered on his adventure to the Himalayas. The words read simply, *Ritual 3: Reward Routinely, Recognize Relentlessly.*

The Ritual

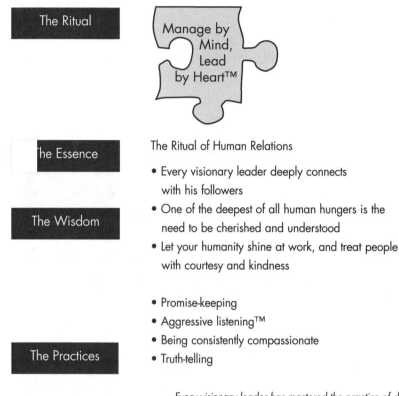

Manage by Mind, Lead by Heart™

The Essence

The Ritual of Human Relations

The Wisdom

- Every visionary leader deeply connects with his followers
- One of the deepest of all human hungers is the need to be cherished and understood
- Let your humanity shine at work, and treat people with courtesy and kindness

- Promise-keeping
- Aggressive listening™
- Being consistently compassionate

The Practices

- Truth-telling

Quotable Quote

Every visionary leader has mastered the practice of deeply connecting to his followers. He has refined the art of clarifying his vision for the benefit of his people in a way that fully engages and stirs them into action. Through their people skills and talents as effective communicators, visionary leaders touch the hearts of their team and earn long-term loyalty. Simply put, when you enrich the relationship, you enhance the leadership.

The Monk Who Sold His F

RITUAL 3

❧

Reward Routinely,
Recognize Relentlessly

The Ritual of Team Unity

Go to the people,
Live among them.
Learn from them.
Love them.
Start with what they know,
Build on what they have.
But of the best leaders,
When their task is accomplished,
Their work is done,
The people will remark,
"We have done it ourselves."

Ancient Eastern saying

WHEN I WAS A KID, my dad would always tell me that we have two ears and one mouth for a reason: to listen twice as much as we speak. Well, for the first time in my entire career, I began to put that lesson into practice. The days following my meeting with Julian in the park brought changes that were nothing short of miraculous. I knew the lessons he had been teaching me had stood the test of time and were sound in nature, but I could not have imagined the impact they would have on my people.

Although I hadn't come close to mastering Ritual 2, I was giving it my fullest effort. I instituted an open-door policy and really meant it. I tried to keep even the smallest promises and commitments I made. I stopped interrupting everyone and became an aggressive listener, as Julian had advised. I now looked for opportunities to perform "minor acts of caring," whether this meant taking a valued manager out to lunch or simply offering a few words of genuine encouragement to a team member who was giving her best. I even started making the disciplines of honesty and openness a key part of my leadership style, sending out e-mails or circulating personally so as to get essential information out to those whom it affected. And what a difference it made.

As with the previous rituals that Julian had shared with me, I knew it would take time before the full power of the second ritual was released. But even within the few weeks of our last meeting, the men and women of GlobalView realized that something big was happening and that they were a big part of it. The programmers soon came up with suggestions to increase our efficiency and innovativeness. After I shared the insight I had gained about enriching human relations with my management team, they instituted a Truth-Comes-First policy and promised the members of their teams they would be "fanatically honest" in all their dealings with them, keeping them in the loop and making certain their voices were heard. It was as if GlobalView was becoming an entirely new company. People started getting to work early and staying late. Just from the conversations I overheard and the way everyone was treating one another, I could sense that everyone was beginning to care again. For me, as their leader, it felt wonderful.

Finally, the night I was to meet Julian at the stadium arrived. As I entered the complex, an usher asked if I needed help. Upon looking at my ticket, he smiled and said, "Welcome to the CivicDome, sir. Let me escort you to your seat. You've got the best location in the house."

As I sat down, I noticed that every seat in our row was occupied, except for the one next to mine. *This must be Julian's seat,* I thought. But where was he? The game was going to start in five minutes and Julian was nowhere in sight. I began to worry. After all, it was not like Julian to be late. He had clearly become a man who practiced what he preached, and I knew he wouldn't want to keep me waiting, especially having whetted my appetite for his profound leadership wisdom during our past two meetings.

Then, two minutes before the game was scheduled to begin, I saw the strangest sight at the other end of the stadium: A man holding a small telescope in one hand and two hot dogs in the other was rushing through the crowd with exceptional speed, the mustard from the hot dogs dripping onto the red robe he wore. When he spotted the place where I was sitting, he let out a yell that attracted the attention of everyone in my vicinity. "Hey, Peter, save that seat! We monks don't get to see many good ball games!" Julian had arrived.

As he sat down, he gently placed his telescope under his chair and handed me the hot dogs. "These are for you, I know you'll love them. The vendor said they are the tastiest he had. Sorry I'm late.

I was watching the stars and lost track of time. It's become quite a passion of mine, you know."

"So I've gathered. What's so special about it?"

"When the time is right, I'll tell you. For now, I suggest you dig into those hot dogs before they get cold. Do you think our guys will win tonight?" he asked, deftly moving on to a new topic.

"I'd be willing to bet on it," I replied. "They're on the longest winning streak in their history. This should be another easy win for them."

As the game got under way, Julian leaned over and asked softly, "Aren't you curious why I asked you to meet me here tonight?"

"Just a little," I replied, understating the truth.

"Well, I thought you'd learn a lot about leadership from watching what's going on here. See the head coach over there?" he said, pointing to a tall bald man, impeccably dressed in a dark blue pinstriped suit, the kind that Julian himself had once favored.

"Yes."

"He embodies the leadership philosophy I want you to adopt. You see, Peter, although he is the team's leader, he doesn't dictate the players' every move. Instead, he coaches, guides, and encourages the players as they liberate their strengths. *Great leaders are great teachers.* That is precisely what you should begin to do. See yourself as a coach, inspiring your team to manifest your future vision and rallying it behind your compelling cause. I'll bet you didn't know that the verb 'to coach' came from the root meaning 'to bring a person from where he is to where he wants to be.' "

"No, I didn't."

"Not only that, but a good coach keeps his or her team highly motivated as it journeys to that place on the horizon. A good coach energizes, challenges, develops, and equips his people. He brings out the very best that they have to offer. He demands that they perform at their peak and then trains them to do so. In this day and age when most organizations suffer from low morale and unmotivated workers, leaders must become skilled coaches to ensure the success of their team."

"So how do I become a great coach and motivate my team?"

"I thought you'd never ask," Julian replied, just as one of the point guards on the home team swished a three-pointer. Suddenly Julian jumped to his feet and started yelling at the top of his lungs: "Way to go! A few more of those babies and we'll be home free!"

I hadn't seen Julian so animated since he'd returned from the Himalayas. On our previous meetings, he'd been so serene and peaceful. Now, amid the excitement of the basketball game, he was on his feet, cheering and clapping like a kid attending the circus for the first time. It was great to see him so happy. He'd been through more turmoil in his life than anyone I'd ever known.

"Sorry about that, Peter. It's just that since my time with the Sages of Sivana, I've learned that every day is a gift. Every day is special and full of tiny blessings. When I was a time-starved, out-of-balance lawyer, I was so busy chasing the brass ring that I lost sight of the simple pleasures of life. I let my family life slip away. I let my friendships slip away. And ultimately I let my health slip away. Sure I made a ton of money and had all the toys any person could dream of. But I wasn't happy. I wasn't fulfilled.

"So now, even though I have few possessions, I find joy in the special moments that every day brings. I look for the extraordinary in the ordinary. And that's why I'm having so much fun tonight. Who knows if I'll ever get to see another game like this."

I was surprised to hear Julian talk in this way. He was so

positive and alive. To hear him speak of his own mortality and the possibility that he might not be around was uncharacteristic of the new Julian Mantle. And I told him so.

"Oh, don't worry, Peter. I plan to live many, many more years. I have so much work left to do in this part of the world. I pledged to Yogi Raman and the other sages that I would spend the rest of my days spreading their message for leadership in business and in life, and I plan to do just that. There are so many more people I can help and so many more things I need to do. The best years of my life still lie ahead of me, my friend. Count on it. All I'm saying is that we must all remember that time slips through our hands like grains of sand, never to return again. Have the courage to embrace and enjoy life as you travel through it."

"Point well taken, Julian. Before your leadership wisdom started to transform our company, I'd become so stressed out I couldn't sleep more than a couple of hours at night. Samantha was worried about it and the kids complained that I was always cranky, which made things even worse. I felt like everything I'd spent my whole life working for was slipping away. My response was to work even harder. But now I know what needs to be done to return GlobalView to peak performance and perfect health. Now I can work *smarter* and begin to enjoy the journey of leadership."

"Good. Okay, back to your question about how one can become a great coach and develop motivated employees. The secret to having highly inspired, loyal workers who will do whatever it takes to help you manifest your vision can be stated in four words. Want to know them?"

"No, I thought I'd get another hot dog," I said with mock sarcasm. "Of course I want to know the secret of highly motivated employees. Doesn't every leader and manager?"

"Well here it is: Reward Routinely, Recognize Relentlessly."

"That's Ritual 3," I said pulling out the third piece of the puzzle, which also had a pattern on it, like the first two.

"Yes, my friend. Ritual 3 in Yogi Raman's ancient leadership system is the ritual of team building. All visionary leaders have made it a daily practice to reward and recognize their employees. They have the wisdom to know that employees who feel appreciated deliver superior results."

"And I'll bet that's another reason that you picked this location for us to meet tonight. Right, Julian? It's all coming together now."

"You're a fast study, Peter. I've always liked that about you. Even in the old days when you were my golf partner, you were always one step ahead of the game. Yes. The head coach is most certainly applying the principle I am sharing with you. He has obviously discovered that when you honor employees, they will come to honor you. He clearly practices the twin leadership disciplines of rewarding and recognizing. That is why his team is so successful."

"Where's the starting point? I'll admit it, I had no idea that rewarding and recognizing employees was so important. I've been so busy with other things that I've never really thought about 'honoring my people,' as you suggest. But I know from my own days as an employee, when I did something right and my manager noticed it, it made me want to perform even better the next time around. Sad to say, in our company, employees don't really hear much from management until they do something wrong. Otherwise, they're pretty much on their own."

"Most companies are like that, Peter. The leadership assumes that the men and women who work for the organization are mature adults who don't require a pat on the back. Managers believe that their job only requires them to spot bad behavior and correct it. They never tell their people about the many positive letters that come in from satisfied customers; instead, they haul their workers into their offices to interrogate them the minute a complaint arrives. In so doing, they unwittingly invite their employees to spend their days trying to avoid bad behavior rather than focusing their energies on doing good work. And rest assured, such companies never grow to world-class status. Would it surprise you to learn that most people in our part of the world go to bed hungry every night?"

"That's impossible, Julian. We live in the land of plenty."

"Well, it's true. Most people go to bed hungry every single night of their lives. Hungry for a little recognition and sincere appreciation for their efforts."

"So what can I do to turn things around? I'm beginning to see the potential of our people peeking through the suits of armor they have donned in response to my old dictatorial leadership style. I am determined to free their strengths and let them be the kind of workers and people they are capable of being. But where do I start?"

"The starting point for motivating your employees is simple: *hunt for good behavior.*"

"What do you mean by that?"

"Well, you said it yourself: At GlobalView you and your managers are constantly looking for bad behavior to correct. The only indicator most of your employees have that they are doing okay is the fact that they have not been fired. Well, that's not good enough. Your people deserve better than that. You need to shift your mind-set and start hunting for people who are doing things right. Get aggressive about finding employees who are performing the way you know they should be. Be like a hunter relentlessly searching for his target. And when you find it, let the rewards and recognition flow freely. *Remember, you always get more of what you reward.*"

"Do you have to acknowledge good behavior immediately?"

"Great question, Peter. Not necessarily, but I'll tell you one thing for sure: the sooner you reward the good behavior, the more likely it is to be repeated. Keep rewarding the kind of behavior you want to see again and again. When you condition your people in this way, they develop a clear sense of your expectations. They will soon realize what success looks like."

"But don't most employees already know what they should be doing? Don't they already know what success looks like? I've always felt that most are simply too lazy to achieve it. In my experience, they just want to make an easy buck and head home as early as possible."

"You are dead wrong," came the blunt reply. "Yogi Raman always told me that almost everyone wants to do good. Each one of us wants to contribute in a positive way and feel that our life has some meaning. We all have dreams and hopes and passions that we pray will be fulfilled one day. But the reality is that most people's ambitions are stifled by the men and women who lead them. They are told what to wear or when to have lunch or how to do their work. Most employees in our part of the world are micro-managed to the point where they feel that it will be detrimental to their careers if they become free thinkers and innovators.

"What you need to start doing, to free the strengths and talents of your people, is to reward the behavior you want to see repeated. Let every single employee know exactly what success looks like by recognizing those who are doing it. You might not believe it, but most workers lack a clear sense of what peak performance means, which further adds to their stress levels. Their leader has never provided them with a model to emulate. Then he or she criticizes them for not doing what they should be doing, making matters even worse.

"I've been in far too many companies where the expectations the leaders have of their employees bear little or no resemblance to employee job descriptions. Visionary leaders define precisely the kinds of results they hope to see from their people and then set them free to realize them. Like I told you earlier, nothing motivates and focuses the mind better than a clear purpose. Once people know where they are going and what is expected of them, they will fulfill their responsibilities."

"But what about when they fail? Surely they need to be punished."

"That leads me to another important point. In underperforming companies, people are so afraid of failing that they never take risks. By never taking risks, they never discover new things. And by never discovering new things, they spend the rest of their lives within a small zone of comfort, doing the same things with the same people in the same way every day. To add insult to injury, management then chastises them for their lack of creativity and innovation. Look, don't get me wrong, Peter, you know I'm a pragmatist; no one is saying that leaders and managers should not correct bad behavior. But don't miss the forest for the trees. Have the vision to understand that failure is essential to success. When one of your people tries something and fails, he or she is simply learning how to succeed. Failures are nothing more than lessons in disguise. They eventually lead us to wisdom and prosperity. Visionary leaders make work environments risk-free. They give their people the freedom to fail. And by doing so, they ultimately succeed."

"Wow, I've never thought of failure like that."

"You might be surprised to learn that at Southwest Airlines — the spectacularly successful company I mentioned earlier — a young manager who came up with an innovative new idea that failed disastrously was actually promoted! The manager had proposed a same-day cargo service that would increase Southwest's revenue by 50 percent. The president personally approved the program and significant sums were spent on advertising and setting up the new operation. Unfortunately, the business never came. But the company's executives understood that while bold risk taking is necessary for massive success, it can also lead to big failures from time to time. It's just a cost of doing business. They ensured that the lesson was well learned and then forged on. By not firing the manager, they sent out a powerful message that innovation and the entrepreneurial spirit was appreciated."

"That's an unbelievable example, Julian."

"It gets even better. Guess how a Southwest employee is recognized when a complimentary letter arrives from a customer?"

"Let's hear it."

"The letter is immediately sent to the employee along with a memo from the president saying, 'I think you're great and my hat's off to you. Keep up the great work. I love you.' "

"Amazing. But I don't know about this loving-your-employees thing."

"At Southwest, the president seizes every opportunity to tell his people that he loves them. The word *love* is not used in a soft, sentimental way, but as an expression of appreciation. However,

---

you don't have to tell your employees that you love them to motivate and inspire them. Just thank them when they do the right thing and forgive them when they make a mistake. To quote the Tibetan proverb that Yogi Raman favored: 'If you are patient in one moment of anger, you will avoid a hundred days of sorrow.'"

"I'd guess that the best way to reward positive behavior and peak performance is with money. True?"

Julian's response was interrupted by the loud sound of the half-time buzzer. Our team was dominating the game and the fans began to applaud warmly. Since Julian had bought courtside seats, we were able to hear what the head coach was saying to the players as they came off the court: "Phenomenal job, guys. We're playing our game just the way we planned it in practice. Keep this up and we're guaranteed a playoff spot. I know you've been on the road for the past two weeks, and I know you guys are darn tired. Let's wrap this one up for our fans."

As the players began walking toward the hallway that led to their locker room, the coach added, 'Hey, guys . . . I'm really proud of you!'"

"Does that answer your question, Peter?" Julian asked.

"Huh?"

"Did that coach just motivate his team?"

"Definitely."

"Did he pull out a sack of money and hand out bills to each player to do it?"

"No," I said with a smile.

"So how did he do it?"

"He praised them. And he did it sincerely. I really felt that he cared about them and felt proud of their excellent performance."

"Exactly. You see, my friend, *praise is free*. Sincere praise can move mountains and revolutionize your entire organization. And it won't cost you a penny. Too many leaders think that bonus checks and cash incentives are the only way to motivate their teams, and since money is tight, they do nothing. Yet, contrary to popular belief, money is not the strongest motivator of human beings. Research shows that people prefer simple praise to almost any other type of reward.

"In one landmark study of 1,500 employees, personalized, instant recognition was found to be the top way to energize staff. Yet only 42 percent received such feedback. In another survey, 58 percent of employees said they seldom received a thank-you note for a job well done even though they said that this form of recognition motivated them the most."

"A simple thank-you note is all they want?"

"Maybe your people want more. You, as their leader, need to make the time to find out. Here's a key lesson: don't reward people according to the way you would like to be rewarded if you were in their shoes. Instead, find out what motivates *them*. Figure out what you and your managers can do to make your employees feel like heroes. Start asking yourself 'the Wow Question.' It's extremely powerful."

"What's 'the Wow Question'?"

"The Wow Question is every leader's best friend. It simply requires that you ask yourself the following: 'What could I do, in terms of rewarding and recognizing my people for excellent work, that would make them say 'Wow' on receiving it?' Remember that timeless truth, Peter: *the way you treat your employees determines the way they will treat your customers.* If you have the discipline to make them feel special, to go 'Wow' on a regular basis, they will do the same for your clients. As I said earlier, giving starts the receiving process.

"Different people must be rewarded in different ways," Julian added. "Gifts need to be customized. Giving a salesperson who hates to fly or is constantly on the road away from her family a trip to Bermuda might not be a great idea. A person who is well paid but working eighteen-hour days just might prefer a few days off over a big bonus check. There was one young guy on my own legal team back when I practiced law who just wanted to be acknowledged for his excellent work in front of the people he worked with. As Yogi Raman said: 'Crack the codes of the people you lead and find out what makes them tick.' Find out what specific things will make them feel good about any success they have achieved. For one it might be a trophy, for another it might be a day pass to a local ski slope. Tailor the reward to suit the person.

"I can still remember Yogi Raman coming into my little hut one day after I had been diligently studying under him and trying very hard to integrate the wisdom of the sages into my own life. 'You have been a very good student, Julian,' he said gently. 'Probably the best one we have ever had. You have been respectful of our customs and shown a very sincere interest in learning our philosophies on leadership and life. Every one of us has grown fond of you. We now see you as a member of our little culture. And though we have few possessions, I would like to give you a small gift as a reward for the progress you made. I would like to give you something that is meaningful, so rather than selecting the gift myself, I thought I'd drop by and find out from you what token would make you happiest.'

"You know, Peter, it was the first time anyone had taken the time to ask me to choose my own reward for a job well done. As a result, I was one happy student. I started studying even harder, just so I wouldn't disappoint this teacher who had invested such faith in me."

"And what did you ask for?"

"I knew you'd want to know. It was something really simple. Inside the temple that stood in the center of the monks' village, there sat a plaque made out of wood. In my quiet moments, I would go in and silently reflect on the words that Yogi Raman had carved onto it. They had great meaning to me. My wish was that Yogi Raman provide me with a similar plaque. He gladly complied, delivering it the very next day."

"What did the words say?" I asked with great interest.

"They were the words of the great Indian philosopher Patanjali. As I have committed them to memory, I can recite them for you:

When you are inspired by some great purpose, some extraordinary project, all of your thoughts break their bonds: Your mind transcends limitations, your consciousness expands in every direction, and you find yourself in a new, great and wonderful world. Dormant forces, faculties and talents become alive, and you discover yourself to be a greater person by far than you ever dreamed yourself to be.

Julian continued, oblivious to the basketball game that had just resumed. "In giving me that plaque, Yogi Raman gave me the reward he knew I wanted —"

"Rather than the reward *he* might have wanted had he been in your shoes," I interjected.

"Exactly. When the visionary leader spots someone in the throes of good behavior, he recognizes her and rewards her as *she* would wish to be rewarded. In this way, the practice of peak performance steadily ebbs through the entire culture of the organization until people don't know any other way to work. That's how you get to world-class status. And it is achievable."

"Okay, so I clearly have to 'hunt for good behavior' around GlobalView. Rather than only looking for people doing things wrong so I can correct them, I must get aggressive about finding people who are doing things right. Then, when I do, I should recognize and reward their efforts, with something tailored to their interests. I'll also get better at the simple act of praising. As you said, most people appreciate praise more than any other form of recognition and yet they rarely receive it. I think I'll make 'Praise Is Free' my new leadership mantra. I'll bet the monks would've liked that one. Mind if I ask you another question?"

"That's what I'm here for, my friend," Julian replied warmly, patting the creases out of the fabric of his long velvet robe.

"My people still need a fair amount of work before they reach peak performance. And yet I know they need to be rewarded and recognized immediately. Should I wait until they improve their skills and are models of good behavior?"

"Brilliant question. You really are digging deep into the wisdom I'm sharing with you. I appreciate this. If you wait until perfect performance arrives, you'll be waiting a long time, maybe forever."

"So what's the secret?"

"The secret is to praise progress and reward results. Hunt for good — not perfect — behavior and get people excited about their improvements. Doing so will be a self-fulfilling prophecy. Peak performance will eventually come because your people will keep getting better and better."

"Kind of like our home team here," I said pointing to the players who had just run down the length of the court on a fast break and scored another two points. "I remember coming to see them when the franchise was brand new. Man, they were pathetic. And yet that wasn't really so long ago."

"And many of those same players have become superstars. The coach praised progress. He found a reason to reward them. And now look at these guys. They are unbelievable," Julian said, jumping to his feet again. His fists were now pumping into the air, and he was yelling words of encouragement to the players, all of whom he knew by name. I never realized that Julian was such a big ball fan. His enthusiasm was contagious.

"Julian, I've got more questions for you."

"Fire away," he said, once again returning to his seat amid the stares of those who had the misfortune to be seated near us.

"I'm not really sure I know what to say when I praise someone. I mean, I've never really done it before. Sure I can say a few quick words like 'nice job' or 'keep it up,' but do you have any other suggestions on effective praising?"

"Praising is a skill that requires study and practice. Every leader needs to get good at it. To get you started, here are a few of the basic praise principles: praise must be specific, it must be immediate, it must be done in public, and it must be sincere. Also, personalize your praise by using the person's first name when making the positive comment. The most beautiful sound in the world to a person is the sound of his or her own name. Oh, and don't fall into the trap that too many managers fall into when they praise."

"Which is?"

"They overpraise. While praise is important, giving it with reckless abandon devalues it, just like printing too much money cheapens the currency."

"Any other specific ideas on motivating my team?"

"Sure. I'll give you some of the best and most cost-effective ones. Posting a personal thank-you note on the employee's door, paying his parking expenses for a month, an annual subscription to the magazine of his choice . . . are simple but proven ways to reward people for excellent performance. Letting an employee attend a meeting for his manager, sending birthday cards, and breaking bread with employees also help to keep them motivated and that show you care. I recently read about one manager who adopted the low-cost but highly effective strategy of filling a large chest full of motivational books, tapes, and videos from respected personal development authors. She called this her 'treasure chest.' When any of her team members deserved to be rewarded, she would walk them over to the chest, in full public view, and encourage them to select something they'd enjoy. I love this idea because it not only rewards good behavior, it allows your people to grow and develop through their exposure to the positive books, tapes, and videos, making them even better performers.

"Remember, Peter, visionary leaders are liberators, not limiters. They know they are duty-bound to help people unlock the best that lies within them and to help them develop a sense of stewardship over their professional and personal lives. They constantly expose their employees to ideas and information that will help them actualize their natural talents and become more independent as thinkers and as people. As the great sage Confucius observed: *'Give a man a fish and you feed him for a day. Teach a man to fish and you feed him for a lifetime.'* Like I told you at the clubhouse that night, leadership is all about freeing people's strengths. When you really get down to it, the actual corporation you call GlobalView isn't much more than a seal and a few pieces of paper spewed out from some corporate lawyer's computer. The true value lies in your people and their potential to help you manifest your grand vision for the future."

"Powerful thoughts. You know, now that I think about it, some of our competitors have some pretty good techniques to energize their employees as well."

"Really?"

"I guess I just didn't understand the power of rewarding and recognition, so I didn't pay much attention to them."

"When the student is ready, the teacher appears," said Julian with a smile as the game drew to a close.

"One of GlobalView's competitors is constantly doing fun things to challenge and stimulate its team. Its sales team always begins meetings by 'celebrating heroes,' going around the table recognizing the salespeople for meeting their goals or for excellence in customer care. Another company has dubbed one office wall 'the victory wall,' placing motivational quotes, testimonial letters, and strategic goals on it for all to see as they pass by. I've even heard about one top Xerox manager who took a ski cap embroidered with the name of a five-star ski resort to every meeting. This 'symbol of victory' served as a powerful reminder of where the team would be vacationing if it met its sales targets."

"Those are fabulous ideas I think you should seriously consider bringing into your organization. And never forget the importance of cultural traditions."

"Run that one by me again," I requested.

"In the Himalayas, the sages had developed a whole series of cultural traditions to keep them unified. Every evening, no matter how busy they were with their philosophical readings or teachings, they would come together to share a simple but delicious meal around a long wooden table. It was really an unbelievable sight to watch these beautifully adorned monks laughing and singing as they ate, savoring the gifts of one another's company and enriching their sense of community. These basketball players do the same thing with their Friday-night pizza parties or their semi-annual family picnics. These are traditions that serve to bring people closer. They encourage teammates to care about one another. They build richer relationships and help people to see themselves as a part of a shared destiny."

"So traditions should become part of our corporate culture?"

"Definitely. Let people get to know one another and let their hair down from time to time. Have family picnics or biweekly submarine-sandwich lunches. Shake the cobwebs out of those huge headquarters you have and get people talking and laughing again. One company I know of even has Crazy Days. Believe me, people not only have a great time, productivity soars. As one wise leader once said, 'Brains, like hearts, go where they are appreciated.' "

"Explain this Crazy Days tradition to me. I've never heard of it."

"In this particular company, a day is designated every quarter as a Crazy Day. It's nothing more than a day designed to let people blow off steam and reduce stress; it boosts morale. For example, one quarter, they designated it as You're Not the Boss Day. The CEO had to make coffee, answer the phones, and work in the warehouse, while some of his employees got to work out of the boss's office and have some fun. This simple idea broke down many of the artificial barriers between management and nonmanagement people and enhanced team spirit. Another quarter, the crazy day was called Corporate Circus Day. Clowns, magicians, and jesters were hired to perform throughout the company's offices, much to the delight of all the employees. Even those passing by the lobby were invited to take part in the spectacle, providing great word-of-mouth promotion about this innovative and people-centered organization. One of the most successful crazy days was Back to the Future Day."

"Sounds intriguing."

"All the employees got together to celebrate their past successes. Personal success stories were posted on the walls of the conference hall that had been rented for the occasion, for everyone to see. Then they all focused on their future goals and brainstormed about the best ways to achieve them.

"The point I'm trying to make with all these examples is that visionary leaders understand that employees who feel they are valued members of an exciting team will go the extra mile to give their best. If you practice Ritual 3 by rewarding routinely and recognizing relentlessly, they will invest their spirits in your organization. And they will begin to see themselves as a part of the larger whole, as an integral part of something special and as an important member of the GlobalView team. That's when your company will become unstoppable. Perhaps Yogi Raman said it best the time he observed that 'when spider webs unite they can tie up a lion.' "

As the crowd filtered out of the stadium, a strange silence filled the air. We had won the game and people were clearly pleased.

But something even more pressing had attracted everyone's attention. Up in the sky, one star had begun to twinkle brightly, illuminating the darkness with an almost magical hue. Although it was almost 11:00 P.M., it appeared as if a rich coat of daylight was waiting to burst through the darkness and envelop the night sky.

I had never seen a phenomenon such as this. Soon the entire crowd was standing still, staring quietly into the sky.

"I can't believe what I'm seeing, Julian," I said, my gaze fixed on the bright star that appeared to be the center of everyone's attention.

"I can," he replied with a knowing smile.

"Does this have something to do with the star you were talking to the other night and that telescope you are carrying?" I asked intently.

"Absolutely. And the time will soon come when I can explain exactly what's going on. When I was in the Himalayas, the sages predicted that this astronomical event would take place. Even I'm surprised at how accurate they were."

Within minutes, the darkness had returned and the glittering star had quietly slipped off into the night. The sight I had just witnessed was astonishing. Although I didn't know anything about astronomy and such natural occurrences, the magnificence of the spectacle was almost overwhelming.

"That was incredible, Julian!"

"The laws of nature are the most powerful laws in the universe," he replied. "They lead you to the truth, Peter. The quality of our lives as leaders is better off by the degree to which we learn from them. Visionary leaders have full knowledge of these laws and align their efforts with them."

"What do you mean?"

"They have the leadership wisdom to understand that 'as you sow, so shall you reap.' They know that the growth of a business follows the same cyclical process as the change of seasons. They are aware that, as in nature, adversity is always followed by opportunity, just as the darkness of the night is always followed by the brightness of the day."

"I've never thought that the laws of nature applied to the business world."

"They sure do, and the leader who recognizes this timeless fact will have an enormous advantage over his or her competition. That's why our next meeting will be in more natural surroundings."

"Where exactly?"

"I'd like us to meet next Sunday in the woods behind Bear Lake."

"You mean the place where all those hunters go?"

"Precisely. Just go to the entrance of the forest. From there, you will see a series of markers that will lead you to the spot where I will continue to share the sages' leadership wisdom with you. I promise that you will not be disappointed."

"What time?"

"At dawn. It's a very special time of the day."

"You're kidding, right?"

"I'm absolutely serious. The dawn is the best part of the day. And I think it's about time you experienced the tranquility it brings. Now I've got to run."

"You're always dashing off, Julian. What's the hurry?"

"I've got to find that star," was the only reply I received as he disappeared into the crowd.

On my way home, my thoughts turned to the wealth of knowledge I had been blessed with on this wonderful evening. I thought about the importance of "rewarding routinely and recognizing relentlessly." I reflected on Julian's point that "praise is free" and how most people go to bed hungry every night, hungry for a little sincere appreciation and respect. I remembered all the men and women of GlobalView who dutifully came into work every morning and spent their days without a word of thanks for the energy they expended. There were the managers and the programmers and the delivery staff who I had never even shown the courtesy of a sincere "Good morning, how are you?" These people were not the root cause of our company's troubles — I was. As Julian had said earlier, great leadership precedes great followership. And I had been far less than the great leader they deserved.

I then contemplated the many creative ways my managers and I could start energizing our people and getting them focused on success. Just thinking about the possibilities and the positive results that would come through their application got me excited. We could set up treasure chests full of motivational books and tapes throughout the headquarters to reward good behavior immediately. We could have submarine-sandwich parties from time to time and set up other traditions so that our people could blow off steam and build stronger bonds. You're Not The Boss Day might be a great way to get the word out that I'm not the same old leader I once was. My mind began to fill with new ideas.

How about leaving nonmanagers in charge while my management team and I headed off for the annual two-day retreat I had decided to organize this year? Why not name boardrooms after top employees? Why not reward a worker who comes up with a new revenue-generating idea with a percentage of the profits it generates, or at the very least with time off? Perhaps the ten best employees of every division could dine with me and the rest of our top executives every quarter? And I would certainly be sending out hundreds of thank-you notes over the coming months. A little praise could go a long way, I realized.

Upon entering the lobby of our luxury high-rise, I reached into the pocket of the light coat I was wearing for my keys, when I felt a foreign object. As I moved into the hallway, a smile came to my face. The light revealed that the object was the next piece of the jigsaw puzzle. Julian must have slipped it in while I was watching the game.

This time the inscription read simply: *Ritual 4: Surrender to Change.*

Chapter 7 Knowledge Summary • Julian's Wisdom in a Nutshell

The Ritual

Reward
Routinely,
Recognize
Relentlessly™

The Essence

The Ritual of Team Unity

The Wisdom

- Great leaders are great teachers and great coaches
- Reward and recognize employees regularly. Give genuine appreciation. You always get more of what you reward.
- Praise is free

The Practices

- Hunt for good behavior
- The "Treasure Chest" and "Victory Wall"
- Symbols of victory and team traditions

Quotable Quote

Visionary leaders understand that employees who feel they are valued members of an exciting team will go the extra mile and give their best. If you practice ritual 2 by rewarding routinely and recognizing relentlessly, they will invest their spirits in your organization. They will begin to see themselves as part of a larger whole. That is when your company will become unstoppable.

The Monk Who Sold His Ferrari

RITUAL 4

Surrender to Change

The Ritual of Adaptability and Change Management

Watch and see the courses of the stars as if you ran with them, and continually dwell in mind upon the changes of the elements into one another; for these imaginations wash away the foulness of life on the ground.

Marcus Aurelius

I COULD NOT BELIEVE I had agreed to meet Julian at this ungodly hour. Not surprisingly, there was no one in sight as I marched up to the entrance to the forest, carrying a Thermos full of coffee and a bag full of pastries, which I hoped Julian might share with me. A remarkable stillness pervaded the scene as I proceeded into the woods. The first rays of daylight peeped through the dense arrangement of trees, guiding me deeper into this natural oasis of calm.

As I walked, the fragrance of pine and cedar tickled my nose, bringing back so many warm memories from my childhood when my father and I would venture into the timberland on long hikes.

Sometimes we would even bring our old canoe and go for long paddles on sun-soaked lakes. Those were some of the best times of my life. I don't know how I got so far away from nature. Right then and there, I resolved to renew the connection. I knew getting back to nature and its inherent peacefulness would allow me to be a better leader and a deeper thinker. As William Wordsworth observed: "When from our better selves we have too long been parted by the hurrying world, sick of its business, of its pleasures tired, how gracious, how benign is solitude." Such wonderful words.

Just then, I noticed what appeared to be a map stuck to the trunk of a large pine tree with a wooden nail. Julian had said there would be markings for me to follow to get to where he would be; this was certainly one of them. I took a moment to study the prescribed route and then ventured farther into the forest. The instructions that had been scribbled onto the map indicated I was to travel north for half a mile. Once there, I would see a small stream that I was to cross and then follow for another mile. This would lead me to what the scribbling said was the Final Resting Place. I had no idea what that meant and didn't wish to worry myself by analyzing it.

I pushed on, growing tired and out of breath after twenty minutes of walking. Sweat dripped from my forehead and onto the soft floor of the forest while my heart beat wildly out of control. But if there was one quality I had always had, it was the fighting spirit. I never gave up, no matter what obstacles I encountered. My father used to tell me there were four elements of one's character that if cultivated, guaranteed success: The first element was discipline; the second, concentration; the third element was patience; and the fourth one, persistence. I always took those words seriously. And so I trudged on.

Suddenly I heard a noise coming from a distant area. It was

soft at first but then grew more noticeable. It sounded like an animal running through the bushes, breaking the small twigs that littered the ground as it moved. Perhaps it was a raccoon or a fox or maybe even a small deer. But then, to my utter surprise, I saw that it was a human figure, swiftly moving among the trees, clutching what appeared to be a long wooden stake! I could not tell if it was a man or a woman, and I was not about to call out and ask. I darted in the opposite direction, genuinely fearing for my safety. After all, there was no help available for miles, and the sight of that sharp wooden stake was less than comforting.

My heart raced even more fiercely and the sweat began to flow like a torrent as I fought my way through the brush, now running as fast as my legs could travel. My Thermos full of coffee and the fresh pastries had been left behind as I cut my way deeper and deeper into the forest. Finally, after running for a little more than half an hour, I realized that the figure was nowhere in sight. I immediately collapsed and lay on the ground, surrounded by bright flowers and small evergreens. Looking up through the trees, I caught glimpses of the blue sky. It was a cloudless summer's day. Perfect really. Too bad I didn't have the energy to move.

My thoughts then turned to Julian. Surely that wasn't him back there with the stake. Why would he have wanted to scare me? And if it was Julian, at least he would have had the courtesy to reveal himself to me. I then grew angry. Here I was, in the middle of a forest notorious for bears, cougars, and wolves and Julian was nowhere in sight. He had said there would be markers that would lead me to him, but I hadn't seen them. To make matters worse, a deranged lunatic with a wooden dagger was hunting for me, and I had no idea how to get back to my four-wheel drive. As a matter of fact, I was totally lost.

Okay. I need to pull myself together, I thought to myself. *I'm the CEO of a two-billion-dollar company. I have a wonderful wife and two great children whom I love deeply and who need me. I'm going to find my way out of this.*

As I stood up, I heard something that offered me the hope I was searching for. It was the sound of a stream, flowing along an area of the forest that was much less densely vegetated. I realized that this must have been the stream that appeared on the map Julian had left for me. If I crossed it, as his instructions had indicated, and followed it for one mile, I would find the Final Resting Place. But which direction was I to travel the one mile in?

I made a guess and headed down the stream. As I progressed, a sense of calmness began to return. Maybe it was the effect of the natural surroundings, the likes of which I had not seen in years. Or perhaps it was because this was the first occasion in a long time that I had taken the time to be by myself.

Eventually, the stream meandered past a particularly rocky area and then along the banks of a large meadow. As I climbed up into this clearing, I saw something very startling. In the center of the meadow stood a small hut made entirely of what appeared to be roses. Surrounding the hut was a vegetable garden and hundreds of exotic flowers. Butterflies flitted through the air, which was laden with a wonderful scent. The whole sight was dazzling. I knew I had found Julian.

"Hello," I called out. "Are you in there, Julian?"

The door of the hut immediately swung open and out came my old friend, beaming. "What took you so long?" he asked. "I've been expecting you for quite a while."

"You wouldn't believe it if I told you. I came here at the crack of dawn, just as you asked. I found your map, read your instructions, and started into the woods. I was having a brilliant time until, all of a sudden, some madman started chasing me with a huge wooden stake. I panicked and started to run until I couldn't run any farther. Luckily I lost him and found that stream. It led me right to you. I think I need a drink to calm down. You wouldn't have any of that expensive Scotch you used to drink, would you?"

"My Scotch days are long gone. And as for the madman, don't worry. I know for certain that he wasn't chasing you," Julian said with a surprising degree of certainty.

"How do you know that?"

"Because it was me. I was running through the woods to get this new stake back to this hut before you arrived. You see, this is my home and I'm planning to do some renovations. I needed the stake to hold up 'the new wing'," he laughed.

"That was you?" I exclaimed. "Julian, I thought I was going to die. Why in God's name didn't you let me know? I could have had a heart attack!"

Julian put his arm around my shoulder in an effort to comfort me. "I almost did. But then a thought came to me. The reason I invited you here today, into this miraculous forest hideaway where I live, is to share the power of Ritual 4 with you. Ritual 4, as you know from my little gift to you the other night, requires you to Surrender to Change.

"I thought that if you were exposed to a little adventure and discomfort, you might have an even better appreciation of the lessons I planned to share. I sincerely apologize if I frightened you. But I knew you'd be okay. As a matter of fact, I was watching out for your safety every step of the way. Now, please come into my home and let's get started. We have an important day of learning ahead of us."

Calming down, I asked, "But what do you mean by surrender to change? And how would getting me to feel uncomfortable be of any benefit?"

"Change is the most dominant force in the business world today, as I'm sure you know. Technology is changing, society is changing, the political landscape is changing, even the way people work is changing. Did you know that in the early 1900s, 85 percent of the workers in our part of the world were in agriculture? Now this field involves less than 3 percent of the work force. And it was recently reported that more information has been produced in the past thirty years than in the entire 5,000-year period before it!"

"I'm not surprised. Change is driving us crazy at GlobalView. By the time one of our products hits the market, it's actually obsolete since we are already testing something even more advanced. People are demanding new methods of doing their work, we are facing more regulation than ever before, our customers' expectations have totally changed, and our competition is now truly global. It seems that by the time we finally come to grips with one new development, ten more come along."

"Precisely. That's why I asked you to come here, to the Final Resting Place, as I jokingly call my little home, to learn about Ritual 4, the ritual of adaptability and change management. You see, every visionary leader goes beyond struggling with change. He or she has the wisdom to realize that if one truly wants to master change, one must *surrender* to it."

"And why would scaring the living daylights out of me help me do this?" I asked, puzzled by the charade Julian had put me through.

"Because the only way to manage change is to become good at managing the unexpected. In order to thrive in the new economy, where intellectual capital is far more valuable than material capital, a leader must master the art of being resilient and reacting to unforeseen challenges with grace, agility, and speed. Sorry to say, my friend, but you failed on all counts."

"I don't follow you."

"Well, my little experiment back there was designed to shake you up and force you to move out of that region of security I've noticed you live your whole life within. From what I gather, you are a creature of routine and never try anything new. You barricade yourself into that massive office of yours and do the same things day in and day out. When something new comes along, a new skill to learn or a new challenge to tackle, you try to delegate it to someone else. At best, you rush to apply the same solutions that have worked in the past to every one of the new problems you encounter. And that's one of the reasons why your company is on the decline rather than seizing the incredible opportunities this new age of business offers.

"Doing the same things every day will not deliver new results. To change the results you are getting, you must change the things you are doing. You must transform the way you are leading. Never forget what Einstein said: 'The significant problems we face cannot be solved at the same level of thinking we were at when we created them.' You must think new, higher, bolder thoughts to manage the change that is bombarding your organization in these topsy-turvy times. You need to become good at tolerating ambiguity and uncertainty. You must embrace the change."

"Is that what you mean by 'surrendering to change'?"

"Yes. For most leaders, there are only two responses to the stress that change inevitably brings: fight or flight. You chose the latter when faced with an unexpected encounter in the woods back there. But there is a third option to managing change, and this is the practice favored by visionary leaders. They surrender to change and, in doing so, use it to their advantage."

"But isn't that a contradiction? If you surrender or submit to change, doesn't that make you the loser?"

"That is the way we think in the West. In the East, however, the sages and Zen masters have adopted a strikingly different mind-set, one that has proven its effectiveness over the centuries."

"And what might that be?"

"They believe that to conquer, one first must yield. Rather than going against the change, one must go with it. As the ancient philosopher Lao-Tzu said: 'Softness triumphs over hardness. What is more malleable is always superior over that which is immovable. This is the principle of controlling things by going along with them, of mastery through adaption.' Rigidly adhering to tradition and outdated ways of doing things will drive a stake right through the heart of your company. Ralph Waldo Emerson said that a foolish consistency is the hobgoblin of little minds. And he was dead right. Be more flexible, more open, and more accepting. Begin to accommodate and align yourself with change. Go with the flow. Be like water," offered Julian. "C'mon. Let's go for a walk."

"Be like water? That's a new one," I said, as we headed down to the stream.

"The nature of water is to flow," Julian observed as he dipped his youthful hand into the bubbling brook. "It goes with the current. It does not resist. It does not hesitate before it yields. But it is also one of the most powerful forces on the earth. Study water and manage the changing currents of modern business like water manages the currents of nature. Rather than viewing change as an adversary, welcome it as a friend. *And then surrender to it.* That's what adaptability is all about."

"Is adaptability that important?"

"Adaptability is one of the most essential leadership skills of our new information-driven world. The leader who can adapt to change and use it to his or her advantage will have a huge competitive edge. But adaptability is more than just going with the change rather than against it. Adaptability is all about recovering from the anxiety and adversity that change initially brings and then having the flexibility to move ahead vigorously. It's about seeing failure as nothing more than market research. It's about understanding that you perfect your abilities by suffering setbacks and that change can allow you and GlobalView to emerge stronger than ever before. It's about persisting until you get to the place where you have determined you must go. Remember, you can't learn to sail without tipping the boat over a few times, and you can't learn to play the piano without hitting a few wrong notes. Success is a numbers game, and setbacks are a part of it. As the Buddhist saying goes: 'The arrow that hits the bull's eye is the result of one hundred misses.' "

"I've always wondered why I've been so resistant to change. Maybe it's in my genes," I joked.

"Actually that's the perfect explanation," Julian replied in a serious tone. "Every human being is genetically programmed to resist change and maintain a state of equilibrium. The condition, known as *homeostasis*, evolved naturally over time as a means by which our ancestors could survive constantly changing conditions. When an environmental change occurs in our own lives, our internal mechanisms jump into play to regulate the new influence and return the body to what biologists call a *steady state*. Essentially, the condition of equilibrium we call homeostasis developed from our need for stability and security. The problem is that the mechanism works to keep things as they are even when more favorable possibilities exist. It doesn't distinguish between change that would make life better and change that would make things worse. It simply resists all change."

"That's fascinating, Julian. You mean to tell me that every single one of us has been genetically designed to resist change?"

"Yes, and that's why people have such a hard time breaking out of their regions of security. They find it hard to adopt new habits, learn a new skill, or cultivate a new attitude. The good news is that homeostats can be reset and change can be embraced. The bad news is that the resetting process always brings stress, pain, and a certain amount of fear with it. Your job, as a visionary leader is to lessen the anxiety by continually reminding your people of why the change is necessary and connecting them to the many benefits that will result from it. Tell them that the change will bring them that much closer to the compelling cause you are all striving toward. Show them how the change will ultimately improve their lives and allow them to be more effective. Make them aware of how the change will help them to serve others and make a deeper contribution. What I'm really saying is help them to master change by giving them the knowledge to change."

"And how do I go about doing that?"

"That brings me to another of the timeless laws of nature, one that is most prevalent in this lush forest I have the privilege to live in — the Law of Environment. A seed grows into a plant only when the soil, moisture, and temperature are favorable. In other words, the environment must be ideal. Similarly, to manage change effectively, you, as a visionary leader, must provide the ideal culture in which people can respond positively to change and grow in the process."

"And what kind of culture would that be?" I asked with great interest.

"You must create a learning culture. You must champion intellectual development. You must foster a workplace that rewards constant learning and skills improvement. You need to let people know that the best way to combat the fear and strain that change invokes is to become knowledgeable about it. *The best antidote for fear is knowledge.* Don't get lazy about learning. The more prepared and informed your people are, the easier it will be for them to accept and thrive on the change. If you really want to succeed in manifesting your vision for the future into reality, help your people become lifelong learners. To stay competitive in this new era, you must let everyone know they need to be continually learning. Create a corporate culture that inspires them to embrace new ideas and information. And share all the information you have. Remember, Peter, in this day and age, *he or she who learns most wins.*"

As Julian climbed back up the bank of the stream and made his way through the lush meadow, he continued to share the leadership wisdom he had acquired about managing change.

"You see, there is joy in change. Without change, there can be no growth. Without change, there can be no improvement. Without change, there would be no progress. Look at this meadow and the forest you came through. It is in a continuous state of change. The leaves fall off the trees and later reappear. The birds hatch as chicks and evolve into adulthood. The seasons change from winter into spring. Even these butterflies are nothing more than caterpillars who learned to change. Understand that change is the way of the world. Change is essential to our evolution as a civilization. It is necessary to our very survival. *Change is*

Robin Sharma

humanity's best friend. Ordinary leaders fight it; visionary leaders delight in it. The ancient philosopher Marcus Aurelius captured these sentiments splendidly when he said: 'Observe always that everything is the result of change, and get used to thinking that there is nothing Nature loves so well as to change existing forms and make new ones like them.' "

"You've transformed the way I view change, Julian. I never would have thought that change is governed by the laws of nature and that it is so central, not only to the success of our company but to the progress of our society. Any other lessons on managing change?"

"One just hopped by," he replied, pointing to a frog with brown spots dotting its dark green back. "My little friend over here is a perfect example of what can happen to you if you decide to wait for large-scale changes to occur in your environment before you make the transition to the new pathways of thought and action that will help you survive."

"How so?"

"Well, if you take a frog and pop it into a pot of boiling water, what do you think will happen?"

"I'd bet it will try to jump out."

"Correct. Now let me offer you a different scenario. Let's say we started the frog off in water that was at room temperature and quietly let him relax in it. Then we gradually started turning up the heat until the water became hotter and hotter. What do you think would happen?"

"Don't tell me the frog would just sit there and do nothing?"

"It sure would, like most organizations do when the change creeping up on them is so incremental that it is easy to ignore. You see, like most companies, the internal system of the frog is only geared to respond and adapt to sudden environmental changes. So when slow changes like the gradual boiling of the water occur, it fails to react. It actually seems to enjoy itself. Then, when it least expects it, it boils to death, yet another casualty of a complacent mind-set."

"Great metaphor, Julian. When did you learn so much about biology?"

"I once dated a high school teacher who taught all that kind of stuff. At the time I found it boring, but now I realize that the laws of nature are essentially the laws of life. And the sooner we come to understand them and apply them in our daily lives, the sooner we will be able to use the changes that are pervading society to our own advantage. Remember, either you align yourself with the laws of nature or you'll find yourself against them."

"And boiled like our friend the frog," I added.

"You got it."

"What else can we do to manage change? I love the lessons you are sharing, Julian. They make so much sense."

"The leadership laws I've revealed to you this morning are all common sense. But most people are just too busy to discover them."

"So true."

"Next, I recommend that you encourage *your employees to become massively competent,*" came the quick reply. "It sort of relates to what I was just saying about being a lifelong learner. But it is even more than that. Being massively competent as an employee means that you stop waiting for management to hold your hand and guide you through the change process. Instead, you assume responsibility for yourself and situations that arise. If there are problems in your division, start thinking about ways that you can fix them. Stop finger-pointing and begin to see yourself as a problem-solver."

"And what can I do, as the leader, to help people develop this sense of maturity and ownership in their work?"

"The secret is to help them increase their ability to add value. People are rewarded in the marketplace according to the value they add to it. A person who flips hamburgers might be more creative than a CEO who makes a nine-figure annual income, but he is obviously adding less value to the market. As a result, he gets paid far less. By helping your people improve their knowledge and competence, you will allow them to add greater value. You will help them realize that organizational change is not a spectator sport, and to survive it; they need to get into the game and make their contributions. In doing so, they will not only raise their levels of confidence and initiative, they will also dramatically reduce the stress they experience."

"How so?"

"One of the greatest stresses associated with high-velocity change occurs when employees fear they will not be able to keep up and will therefore be seen as less than employable. And yet most organizations still don't see the value of constant leadership and skills development training. Corporations regularly spend 50 to 70 percent of their money on people's salaries and yet invest less than 1 percent of their budgets on training them to improve their abilities. It makes no sense. By constantly investing in your people, sending them to training seminars and exposing them to the latest business books, you will sharpen their skills, develop their talents, and help them to see that they can actually assume a leading role in effecting change within the organization. You will help them turn weaknesses into strengths. 'Empty the pennies from your purse into your mind and your mind will fill your purse with dollars and keep it full forever,' said Ben Franklin, while Abe Lincoln noted that 'one's security in life comes from doing something uncommonly well.' Spend the money required to make your people leaders in their field. Understand that employee development is an investment, not an expense. Know that *the growth of your company is directly proportional to the growth of your people.* By helping your people become so good at what they do that they become indispensable, you will not only boost productivity, you will gain loyalty."

"That's so true, Julian. We have this one young guy who started out as a shipping clerk. He was a really nice kid — one of the few people in the company I connected to in any real way — and from time to time I would have a quick chat with him. He told me that he really wanted to try his hand at computer programming but lacked the skills. So I sent him through a training program at no cost to him. Pretty soon, at lunchtime he was hanging around with the other programmers and giving them a hand. It became clear that the kid was gifted, so one of my managers gave him a job writing software programs."

"So where is he now?"

"He's our number-one programmer. One of our competitors tried to lure him away with the incentive of a much higher income, but he turned the offer down. Said he was happy just where he is. I wish all my team felt that way."

"Maybe they would if you invested in them as you did in the young hotshot. You rewarded him with the chance to develop himself; he, in turn, rewarded you with his trust. See, another reason why people resist change is that they simply don't trust the leadership. They don't believe their managers and supervisors have their best interests in mind. People challenge those who lead egocentrically. Helping your employees to become massively competent will change all that. If you see yourself as a builder of people, they will see that you are committed to them. One very successful company I used to represent allotted only four days of the week for work."

"What about the fifth?"

"It reserved that for training its people."

"Unbelievable."

"Having emphasized the importance of continuous improvement of your people, never forget the forest for the trees."

"What do you mean?"

"All too often well-intentioned leaders bring in the speakers, send their team members to seminars, invest in the latest business books and tapes, but they fail to remember the most important thing."

"Which is?"

"*Knowledge that remains unapplied is worthless.* Success is not determined by what you know. Many employees realize what things they need to do to help the organization prosper. Lasting success comes only through acting on what you know, putting it into practice. To become a truly world-class company, you and your people must move from learning to doing and from wishing to being. I still recall that in his little hut Yogi Raman had a saying that reminded him of the importance of acting on positive intentions."

"What did it say?"

"It read: 'Spring has past, summer has gone and winter is here. And the song that I meant to sing is still unsung. I have spent my days stringing and unstringing my instrument.' I believe those words kept him connected to the fact that time is passing, and now is the time to translate your good ideas into real results." Julian then looked up at the sky, staring at one particular area and muttering something that sounded like, "I'll be looking for you soon, my friend." By now, I'd grown used to his sometimes odd behavior and chalked it up to his exposure to the otherworldly sages in the Himalayas.

"Okay, a final thought before we call it a morning," he continued, returning his attention to me. "I know you must be tired from all the excitement earlier, and I've got some things I have to attend to today. The last of the natural laws that will help you master change is the one I mentioned to you last time we met: *as you sow, so shall you reap*. It's the ancient Law of the Harvest."

Julian then walked me over to his vegetable garden. "I spend some time every morning cultivating my garden. I show it great respect since its produce feeds me. I lovingly till the soil, offer it water, and keep it clear of weeds. I have learned that the more I care for it, the more it will care for me. These vegetables are another one of the reasons I look as young as I do."

Julian then reached over and pulled out a fresh bunch of carrots. I was amazed at how big they were and told him so.

"Want to take some of these home with you?"

"Sure, Samantha would love them."

"You see, Peter, our minds are very much like this garden. If we care for them, if we cultivate them and if we put in only the best nourishment, they will produce a bounty that will lead us to success. The problem with most people is that they let anything in. They start their days reading the negative stories in the newspaper. Then they have negative thoughts while waiting in traffic. Once at work, they focus on all the negative things rather than having the wisdom to search for the positives. And then, at the end of the day, after filling their minds with nothing but the worst input, they wonder why they feel so tired and miserable. Remember, your mind can either be your best friend or your worst enemy. Don't let the weeds take over. Manage your inner morale. Assume full responsibility for attitude control. As you sow, so shall you reap."

"My father used to tell me that one," I said quietly.

"It sounds like he was a wise man," noted Julian. "You see, when you really get down to it, leaders don't lead companies. They don't even lead people. What they really lead and inspire are *attitudes.* They show their people the higher reality that waits for them on the horizon and then equip them with the enthusiasm and skills they need to get there. So place a premium on positive thinking in your organization. Believe me, it's not 'soft stuff' like many unenlightened leaders and managers will tell you. An inspired, energized mind-set is the very essence of success.

"I'll tell you something else," Julian added. *"In this new era of business you are privileged to live in, ideas are the true commodity of success. How far you go will be determined by how well you think.* As Disraeli said, 'Nurture your mind with great thoughts for you will never go any higher than you think.' "

"That's a really good point, Julian. What you mean is that, when all is said and done, the only limitations to our success lie within our thinking."

"Exactly. Think about it for a second. Every great discovery, achievement, or invention began as a simple thought in the mind of an inspired man or woman. Edison's idea to create the incandescent light bulb, or Salk's desire to develop a vaccine to immunize against polio, or Gandhi's drive to deliver his people to freedom all began as a single thought in their minds. Nothing more, nothing less. Are you beginning to see the power that lies within the ten-pound mass resting between your shoulders and the shoulders of your people?"

"Yes."

"So one of the best change-management disciplines you can possibly follow is to start conditioning your mind and the minds of your people to view all the upheaval that is going on as one huge opportunity to learn, grow, and succeed. Train them to constantly see the good in every circumstance, the possibilities where others see adversity. Visionary leaders show their people a higher, more inspiring reality when the rest of the world sees darkness," Julian said, his voice filled with passion. "As Helen Keller said, 'No pessimist ever discovered the secrets of the stars, or sailed to an uncharted land, or opened a new heaven to the human spirit.'

"Oh, and by the way," Julian added, "I also suggest you tell your people to become inverse paranoids. It will really boost productivity and morale."

"What's an inverse paranoid?"

"An inverse paranoid is someone who believes the world is conspiring to do something *good* to him or her. And as the great Harvard psychologist William James once said, 'Belief creates the actual fact.' "

"I like that one."

"It's true, Peter. Our expectations create our reality. Success in business and in life is a self-fulfilling prophecy. Thoughts have power — never forget this timeless natural law. You see, thinking is a lot like walking down these footpaths," said Julian, as he pointed to an intricate series of paths leading to different locations, away from his hut, "Every day, you have a choice as to which path you will take. Take one path, and it is certain to take you to one destination. Choose another, and it will take you to an entirely different place. If there's one thing the sages taught, it's that the quality of your leadership can ultimately be traced back to the quality of your choices."

"Really?"

"Sure. The ageless law of cause and effect always prevails. The level of your success will, at the end of the day, boil down to what activities and initiatives you have chosen to focus on. What people you have chosen to surround yourself with. What opportunities you and GlobalView have chosen to seize. What books you have chosen to read."

"And what thoughts I have chosen to allow into the garden of my mind," I said, fully grasping the point Julian was making about the power of choice.

"Excellent, Peter. I couldn't have asked for a better student, you know," replied Julian. "So like I say, thinking is like walking down these footpaths. If you have the self-discipline to choose the right one, it will take you to where you are hoping to go. But if you take the wrong one, you can be certain you will never reach your predetermined destination. And that's what negative thinking is all about. A stressful thought enters your mind, and rather than moving on to another more enlightening one, you walk down that path. And just like on these footpaths, the more times you walk down that negative path, the more familiar it will become. The more it will feel like this is the path for you. And we both know where that kind of mind-set will lead you in this era of change. Yogi Raman shared with me the fact that the Sanskrit word for 'funeral pyre' appears strikingly similar to the word for 'worry.' "

"Amazing."

"Actually it's not when you think about it. The two are related."

"Really?"

"Sure. *The funeral pyre burns the dead while worry burns the living.* So when a disempowering thought slips into your mind, refuse to empower it by lending it further energy. Refuse to go down that path and quickly move on. It will make a world of difference in the way you think and feel."

"Mark Twain used to say, 'I've had a lot of trouble in my life, some of which actually happened.' Now I finally understand what he meant by it," I observed.

"I'll have to remember that one, Peter. As you can tell, I love to quote the wisdom of great thinkers and that's a good one."

As Julian led me through the forest back to where my four-wheel drive rested, I contemplated all the changes GlobalView was going through and how I might apply his leadership wisdom to use them to our advantage. In our short time together, I began to see that change really was nature's way of ensuring that things evolved and improved. Rather than fighting it, I now understood I had to surrender to it and align myself with it if I hoped to meet with success. I had to adopt a new, more enlightened worldview and focus on the tremendous opportunities presented by this new era of business we found ourselves in. I had to stop blaming change and become a part of it. As Thomas Fuller once observed: "Accusing the times is but excusing ourselves." My managers and I had to stop being so reactive and become more adaptive. We had to become visionary leaders. It had been an extraordinary morning, and I told Julian so.

"The best is yet to come, my friend. You won't believe where our next meeting will take place. I have quite a session planned for you," he chuckled.

"I can't wait," I replied, shaking my head from side to side. "I better make sure all my health insurance is paid up. Learning the rituals of visionary leaders has been quite an adventure! So where will it be?"

"At the Yaleford Military Base," came the straightforward reply.

"You're kidding, right?"

"No. It's the perfect place for me to reveal the fifth ritual of the timeless leadership system that Yogi Raman shared with me deep within the Himalayas. Let's meet at 8:00 P.M. next Friday night."

"Sure. Do I get a quick preview?" I asked, unable to control my curiosity.

"Sure, why not. Have a look for yourself," Julian said as he reached into his robe and pulled out yet another of the wooden puzzle pieces I now looked forward to receiving. I had discovered that the previous ones all fit together perfectly and were starting to form some sort of image. I was sure that this new addition would add further clarity to the shape that was forming.

"I can't see any letters on this one, Julian. What's wrong?"

"It's upside down, my friend," he offered with a grin.

Sure enough, when I rotated the piece I saw the markings I had hoped for, the next clue to how I could transform my leadership and jump-start our organization. The inscription read only, *Ritual 5: Focus on the Worthy.*

Chapter 8 Knowledge Summary • Julian's Wisdom in a Nutshell

The Ritual

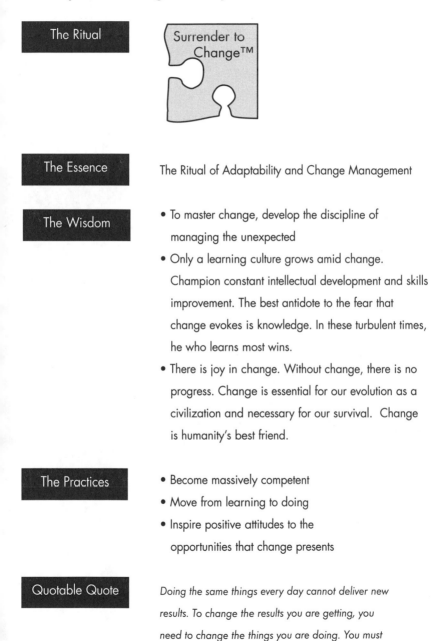

Surrender to Change™

The Essence

The Ritual of Adaptability and Change Management

The Wisdom

- To master change, develop the discipline of managing the unexpected
- Only a learning culture grows amid change. Champion constant intellectual development and skills improvement. The best antidote to the fear that change evokes is knowledge. In these turbulent times, he who learns most wins.
- There is joy in change. Without change, there is no progress. Change is essential for our evolution as a civilization and necessary for our survival. Change is humanity's best friend.

The Practices

- Become massively competent
- Move from learning to doing
- Inspire positive attitudes to the opportunities that change presents

Quotable Quote

Doing the same things every day cannot deliver new results. To change the results you are getting, you need to change the things you are doing. You must transform the way you are leading.

The Monk Who Sold His Ferrari

RITUAL 5

꧁꧂

Focus on the Worthy

CHAPTER NINE

The Ritual of Personal Effectiveness

Your task it is, amid confusion, rush and noise, to grasp the lasting calm and meaningful and finding it anew, to hold and treasure it.

Paul Hindemith

IT HAD BEEN MANY YEARS since I had been to the old military base just off County Road Number 27. My father used to take me there as a boy. For hours we would sit on the high hill that overlooked the compound and watch the soldiers performing their drills with pinpoint accuracy. I still don't know what he found so absorbing about the spectacle. Maybe it was the pageantry. Perhaps it was the precision of the exercises. Maybe it was the simple fact that the outing offered him rare time alone with his little boy. One thing was for certain, however, I sure did miss him.

As I parked my BMW in the empty lot, I scanned the grounds for Julian. It was 8:00 P.M. and I was right on time, but my old friend was nowhere in sight. The only people I could see were young cadets marching across the field with their youthful-looking drill sergeant shouting commands at the top of his lungs.

For a while the soldiers remained at the center of the grassy area, but then they started marching in my direction. I wondered why they would be coming near the parking lot when they had the whole compound to practice their routines. Soon it became obvious that they were headed straight for me. As the cadets drew closer, their strides quickened. I remained in my spot, not moving a muscle. As they neared, I could see that many of them were smiling. Some were even laughing as streams of sweat trickled down their faces, the salty by-products of rigorous exercise and the evening sun.

I still couldn't see the sergeant who was running the show, but I decided I would give him a piece of my mind. After all, these were the people who were charged with protecting this great country, and their drills should have been taken seriously. Surely they had better things to do than harass an innocent civilian. Then the cadets all stopped. While they kept their smiles, none of them looked at me, preferring to fix their gaze on a point off in the distance. I decided I would take the initiative, so I started walking down the line of people, searching for their leader.

Finally I reached the end. Although his face was shielded by the brim of the hat he wore, I could see that he was in perfect shape: tall, lanky, and trim, with a ramrod-straight posture to match.

"What's going on here?" I questioned in the gruff tone that once made my employees twitch. "I just pulled into the parking lot to meet a friend. Why have you marched your people over to me? I wasn't in your way."

"We have come to interrogate you," came the firm reply. "There is a question we must ask you. If you answer it correctly, you are free to do as you please. If, on the other hand, you give us the wrong answer, we will have to take you into custody."

Surely this had to be a joke. All I had done was drive into their parking lot. I was the CEO of one of the largest corporations in the country. I paid my taxes and followed the law. While I might not have been a great leader, my sins did not warrant incarceration.

"Look, I don't know what this is all about, but I think you have the wrong guy. I'm a businessman. I run a big software company. I'm here to meet an old friend who was supposed to be here at 8:00 P.M. It's not like him to be late. Perhaps you and your men saw him on the grounds. You couldn't have missed him. He would have been wearing a red monk's robe."

The men all started laughing, quietly at first and then much louder. The drill sergeant maintained his composure and continued, "I still need to ask you this one question. As I say, if you answer it correctly, you can do what you want to do."

"Okay, let's hear it," I replied in utter frustration.

"Did you bring the fifth piece of the puzzle?" asked the soldier.

"I beg your pardon?" I stuttered.

"You heard me, Peter. Did you bring the fifth piece of the puzzle? How can we continue with Yogi Raman's formula for visionary leadership if you don't have the next piece of the puzzle?"

I immediately reached over and ripped the long-brimmed hat off the man's head. I was shocked to see who it was. It was Julian! He swiftly slapped me on the back and laughed while the recruits, who were obviously in on his elaborately crafted ploy, began to cheer.

"Welcome to Yaleford Military Base, Peter!"

"You're unbelievable, Julian. How did you get everyone to go along with you? And what happened to your robe? I thought you never took it off."

"Only for special occasions like this," he smirked. "The base commander and I are old friends. We went to Harvard together. He owed me a favor and I decided this was the time to call it in."

The cadets returned to formation and headed back to the barracks while Julian and I walked to the center of the field, just as the sun was setting on another beautiful summer's day. By now, I had calmed down and had begun to see the humor in Julian's prank.

"I did bring the fifth piece of the puzzle, though," I said.

"Great. Tonight's lesson is another essential one if you truly hope to enrich your leadership."

"And what exactly does 'Focus on the Worthy' mean?"

"Let's say I had the power to grant you any wish. What would you ask for?"

"That's easy. Like most other leaders and managers I know, I'd love to have more time. Just give me an extra hour a day and I'd be one happy man. With all the meetings I have to attend, all the reports I have to read and all the problems I have to solve, I never seem to have time to do the important things that would really allow GlobalView to excel. I mean, I can't remember the last time I had a few hours to simply sit back and strategize our future. There always seem to be a hundred tiny brush fires to put out, and the deeper issues that I know I need to think about always get put over to another day. So my wish would definitely be for more time."

"You've got it," replied Julian.

"Just like that?"

"Well, I already told you how to get it: Focus on the worthy. The secret of having more time to concentrate on the necessary things is to have the courage to neglect those that are unnecessary."

"Is it really that simple?"

"It is. It's the habit that every visionary leader before you has mastered since time immemorial. One day, the great inventor Thomas Edison was asked the secret behind his extraordinary success. He pondered for a moment and then replied, 'The ability to apply your physical and mental abilities to one problem incessantly without growing weary.' You do something all day long, don't you? Everyone does. If you get up at 7:00 A.M. and go to bed at 11:00 P.M., you have put in sixteen good hours, and it is certain that most people have been doing something all that time. *The only trouble is that they devote their time to a great many things, while I devote mine to only one. If they took the time in question and applied it to one object, they would succeed.*

"Visionary leaders have a clear sense of their destination and exactly what things they need to accomplish to reach it," continued Julian. "They know intimately their high-yield activities, those that result in the progress they need to make in order to get to where they want to go. Anything else is a waste of their precious time and they disregard it. You see, Peter, *the real secret of personal effectiveness is concentration of purpose.* As Emerson stated: 'Concentration is the secret of strength in war, in trade; in short in the management of human affairs.' In leadership, there are activities that are worthy of your energy and attention, and there are activities that are unworthy of them. Once you figure out which ones to focus on and then have the self-discipline to do it, your effectiveness as a leader will be liberated."

"In business school I remember reading Peter Drucker's admonition to 'switch from being busy to achieving results,' " I offered.

"Correct. And he also wrote that 'there is nothing so useless as doing efficiently that which should not be done at all.' The philosopher Confucius made the point even more simply when he said: 'The man who chases two rabbits catches neither.' Yogi Raman put it yet another way when he told me, *'The person who tries to do everything achieves nothing.' So the real secret to getting things done is knowing what things need to remain undone.* And that's what Ritual 5 is all about, it's the ritual of personal effectiveness. To find the time to do what you should be doing in order to get where you are going, you must have the leadership discipline to focus on the worthy. You must develop a sense of tunnel vision for your highest leadership priorities. Once you do, you will never be the same again."

"Can you give me an example of worthy activities?"

"Only you can decide on those for sure. Let me just say that any pursuit that somehow advances you closer to the vision you have of the future is time well spent. Any task that actually gives you a solid return on the time invested and gets you nearer to the outcome you are ultimately aiming for should be considered. It's like the old law you must have learned in business school that held that 20 percent of your activities deliver 80 percent of your production. So focus on the things that count, those pursuits that are worthy. And the magic of the concept is that by saying yes to the worthy, you implicitly say no to the unnecessary. You automatically simplify your leadership and streamline your life."

"Simplify my leadership. I really like the sound of that one."

"It's like a Zen monk once said: 'Most people I know try to become more clever every day, whereas I attempt to become more simple and uncomplicated every day.' The simpler your leadership focus, the more effective you will be."

"Okay, let me try to come up with some of those high-yield activities that will link me to my mission and advance the compelling cause that I've come up with since we met a few weeks ago. What if I spend time communicating my vision and helping my people understand how achieving it will help us touch the lives of others?" "Definitely high-yield." Good answer," Julian remarked, clapping his hands like a game-show host.

"How about spending time with my managers asking one another how we can motivate our people by Rewarding Routinely and Recognizing Relentlessly?"

"Well done, Peter. Another fine idea."

Sensing I had the gist of the leadership philosophy Julian was sharing with me, I rushed through a partial list of activities that I realized would transform my leadership effectiveness: regular periods of strategic thinking, consistent preparation and planning, professional and personal development and relationship building.

"And the funny thing is," added Julian, "that the more time you spend on these high-yield activities, the less time you will have to spend on all those crazy little emergencies you've complained of that seem to suck away your precious time."

"How so?"

"Just think about it. If you spend your days communicating your message and building richer relationships rather than micromanaging as most leaders do, there will be fewer misunderstandings and less conflict. By spending more time praising and rewarding your people for behavior you want to see repeated, quality, productivity, and efficiency will skyrocket. Again, saving you time. And if you devote more time to strategic thinking and improving your own knowledge base, you will become a better thinker, making wiser decisions in the process. Again, smarter decisions mean fewer crises, which means that you save time. It's actually a brilliant concept that the sages came up with. I still can't believe how powerful it is."

"Why do you think most of us don't apply it?"

"Well, first, most people are so busy that they've never stepped back to consider how they could improve their own effectiveness. But as Thoreau said: 'It is not enough to be busy, so are the ants. The real question is what are you so busy about?' Most people are ant chasers rather than elephant hunters if you get my metaphor; they spend their days concentrating on trifles that don't contribute to the advancement of their objectives rather than going after the big game that would really get them to their professional and personal goals. They just don't focus on the things that count. The second reason is that they don't know where to start. They've been squandering their time for so long that they have no idea how to turn things around."

"I'm all ears."

"The trick is to have a system. Effective systems ensure inevitable results. What I'm really trying to tell you is that if you want to focus on the worthy, *you must first ritualize the worthy.* You need a system that will allow you to integrate your high-leverage activities into your day, every day. Only in this way will you be able to shield your hours from the low-impact activities which, over time, will destroy your leadership."

"Did Yogi Raman give you a system to ritualize the worthy?"

"He sure did. It's called the Time Model for Visionary Leadership. Quite simply, it is the most effective method I have ever come across for time leadership."

"You mean time management."

"No, I mean time leadership. Every sane person in business today has some way to manage time. But only the visionaries have discovered how to *lead* their time. *Visionary leaders have the wisdom to understand that if you don't lead your time, it will lead you.*

"Interesting thought," I noted. "So how does this Time Model for Visionary Leadership work? It sounds complicated."

"Actually it's incredibly simple once you get the hang of it. 'Simplicity is the highest form of elegance,' my Himalayan friends would say. The first thing you must do is set aside a period of time for what Yogi Raman called 'a weekly planning practice.' This might be a half-hour on a Sunday night or first thing on a Monday morning. My recommendation to you is that you do it on Sunday night. The weekend's activities have come to an end, and it is easier to find a little quiet time for yourself."

"Easier than on Monday morning, that's for certain."

"True. Once you've figured out when you're going to do your planning every week, there are five key steps you must follow to ritualize the worthy and ensure that every action you take during the coming week brings you closer to your ultimate goal. Step One is to revisit your future vision. Silently consider both the vision statement you have developed not only for your company but also for your life. Envision what ultimate success will look like both professionally and personally. This will remind you of where you are going and renew your sense of purpose. Deeply connect to what GlobalView will be when you reach your destination and how your family life will look once you become the kind of husband and loving father you hope to be. Revisiting your vividly imagined future will keep you inspired and focused on the things that count."

"I'm with you so far. What comes next?"

"Step Two then requires you to review the annual victories you have determined are worthy of achieving this year."

"Exactly what are annual victories?"

"They are the objectives you have set for yourself after figuring out what uses of your time will have the most impact on the advancement of your future vision during the current year. They are your annual goals. By reconnecting with them, you will remind yourself of your best practices, those pursuits that are certain to deliver you and your company to your predetermined destination. And you will begin to have a much clearer sense of those low-yield activities that wise leaders never even go near. If there's one thing that can be said about the new era of business we find ourselves in, it's that leaders are facing more choices than ever before.

"On any given day," Julian continued, "there are a hundred possible opportunities to consider, or a hundred new changes to implement, or one hundred possible trade magazines to read. There are one hundred possible things to do at the office, and one hundred possible channels to watch on TV, and one hundred possible books to read in whatever spare time you have. We are being overwhelmed by choice. Just the other day I went into the grocery store and noticed there were fifteen different kinds of bread! The only way to survive the incredible barrage of choice coming at us is to have a predetermined game plan. If you have one, you will have created a framework that will allow you to select only those choices that will advance your purpose. You will begin to be the master of all the choices rather than their servant. As the novelist Saul Bellow once wrote: 'A plan relieves you of the torment of choice.' "

"That's a powerful way of putting it."

"And Victor Hugo said this about the importance of having clearly defined goals and a firm plan: 'He who every morning plans the transactions of the day and follows out that plan carries a thread that will guide him through the labyrinth of the most busy day. The orderly arrangement of his time is like a ray of light which darts itself through all his occupations. But where no plan is laid, where the disposal of time is surrendered merrily to the chance of incidents, all things lie huddled together in one chaos, which admits of neither distribution nor review.'

"My point is that smart leaders have already predetermined the best uses of their time. And in so doing, they are better able to manage the army of choices they are faced with. It's easy to say no to something when there's a better thing to do. As I said earlier, the secret to getting things done is knowing what to leave undone. This is the ancient Law of Planned Neglect and it is a law that has been mastered by every visionary leader since the beginning of time."

"This is really intriguing, Julian. What you are sharing with me is an almost scientific process to get important things done in an age where there are too many things to do."

"That's right, and that's precisely why I say that the model helps you to ritualize the worthy."

"And Step Three in the process?" I inquired.

"Once you have connected to your future vision, either by imagining it in your mind's eye or reviewing it on paper, and taken a quick glance at the specific victories you plan to achieve this year, you must ask yourself a very powerful question: 'What minor victories or little goals must I accomplish *over the next seven days* for me to feel that this week has advanced me in the direction of both my professional and personal vision?' Your answer will give you what Yogi Raman called a series of 'weekly wins.' Those goals are what you must focus on through the week. They will allow you to have the self-discipline to sacrifice the good for the best. These weekly objectives will concentrate your energy and attention on the worthy."

"What do you mean when you say coming up with my weekly wins will help me sacrifice the good for the best?"

"Well, *all too often leaders let their good intentions dominate their best ones.* Rather than constantly asking themselves whether they are making the *best* possible use of their time, they focus on activities that are simply *good* uses of their time. And believe me, there's a big difference. *Visionary leaders focus on the best and delegate the rest.* Never forget that."

"And by focusing on the best uses of my time through your weekly wins concept, every day of the week and the week itself will serve some purpose, right?"

"Yes. Most people let their days slip by without realizing that the days slip into weeks and the weeks slip into months and the months slip into years. They put second things first and major in the minor. Pretty soon your whole life has slipped by simply because you didn't take charge of your days. As the sages used to tell me: *'If you don't act on life, life will act on you.'* "

"That's so true," I replied, growing reflective.

"No only that, they also believed that every day is nothing but a miniature version of your life. In life, at the beginning you are born and at the end you die. Similarly, in your days, in the morning you wake up and at night you go to sleep. But what you do in between those daily periods determines, in a very real way, whether your life will be one that is well lived or wasted. Never forget the importance of each and every one of your days, Peter. *As you live your days, so you live your life.* Don't waste even a single one of them. The past is history and the future is just a figment. This day, the present, is really all you have."

"So setting weekly wins each week will bring me closer to my annual victories, which, in turn, will advance me in the direction of my future vision, right?"

"Exactly."

"Wow. That means that if I follow this simple process, every single one of my weeks will count for something."

"Right. And your life begins to be flooded with a sense of fulfillment and energy because you know you are steadily moving toward the place you have dreamed of being," noted Julian.

"So once I've determined my weekly wins, what comes next?"

"Step Four of the Time Model for Visionary Leadership requires you to integrate the weekly wins you have promised yourself you will achieve over the coming seven days into your daily schedule. You see, by actually writing your weekly goals into your schedule, much as you would a meeting with your best customer, you will be sure to follow through on them. By carving out specific times to achieve your weekly wins before less worthy things get scheduled, you will be certain to give your priorities the priority they deserve. Remember this time leadership truth, *if your priorities don't get put into your planner, other peoples' priorities will get put into your planner.* And by practicing the simple time planning discipline I am suggesting, every one of your days will link you that much closer to your future vision. It's the ultimate tool for a life of achievement."

"I guess the real challenge would be to stick to the plan once the days start getting busy, as mine always do."

"That's right. *The golden key to time leadership is really doing what you planned to do, when you planned to do it.* Like every other one of the leadership philosophies I've shared with you, the starting point is self-discipline."

"Really?"

"Absolutely. Self-discipline is the DNA of visionary leadership. Self-discipline is the common trait of the best of the best. Self-discipline is what allows a leader to go beyond knowing to doing. Like I told you, it's not what you know that's important. Success comes from *acting* on what you know — and self-discipline is what stirs visionary leaders into action."

My father used to talk about the importance of discipline and self-control when I was growing up. I still remember him telling me that *"the tougher you are on yourself, the easier life will be on you."* And, to use Julian's terminology, my dad's "video was in synch with his audio." He would wake up at 5:00 A.M. every day of the week and go out for his daily run. He didn't smoke or drink and lived a simple but honorable life. He never spoke ill of others and always kept his promises. He truly believed that the dissatisfaction most people experienced in their lives could be traced back to a lack of discipline, whether that meant not having the self-control to eat well, or not nurturing key relationships, or not having the courage to take some risks and follow one's dreams. *Maybe that's why he loved bringing me to this military base,* I thought. These soldiers are models of discipline. They are trained to get things done and never back down from what they know to be right. They come up with a plan and then have the inner power to follow it to completion. I shared my thoughts with Julian.

"That's precisely why I brought you here this evening," he replied, delighted with my insight. "The ritual of 'focusing on the worthy' requires tremendous self-discipline and inner conviction. *The greatest battles we fight take place within ourselves.* These soldiers and their commitment to keeping themselves on a short leash, to getting tough with themselves, will always remind you of that. You see, Peter, it's a complete waste of time to go through the planning process I'm sharing with you and schedule periods to carry out your highest-yield activities and then, when push comes to shove, let something else intrude. *There's no point in strategic planning if you never carry out the plan.* I know it isn't always easy to do what you planned to do when there are so many distractions that might be so much easier to pursue. But you must do what you know to be right. 'The successful person has the habit of doing the things failures don't like to do,' remarked essayist and thinker E. M. Gray. 'They don't like doing them either necessarily. But their disliking is subordinated to the strength of their purpose.' The nineteenth-century English writer Thomas Henry Huxley arrived at a similar conclusion noting, 'Perhaps the most valuable result of all education is the ability to make yourself do the thing you have to do, when it ought to be done, whether you like it or not.' "

"Those are absolutely brilliant observations, Julian."

"That's what self-discipline and personal courage are all about — doing the things we must do, even if we don't like doing them. *Deferring those things that are easy to do and preferring those things that are honorable and right to do.* I'm not saying you shouldn't be flexible. If something unexpected comes up, by all means attend to it if it's the best use of your time at that particular moment. Like I said when we were discussing how to manage change, flexibility is one of the most important disciplines for visionary leadership. But just make sure you focus the majority of your time on the worthy things, on the right things."

"So back to the Time Model for Visionary Leadership. I just write the weekly wins I have to come up with into my daily planner and then have the courage and self-discipline to stick to them?"

"Yes and no."

"C'mon, Julian. I'm serious. I really need to learn this process. I have a feeling the sages were onto something very powerful."

"I say yes because you must note your weekly wins into your organizer. I say no because it's actually a little more sophisticated than that. I call the technique of integrating your weekly wins into your days *strategic time blocking.*"

"Sounds fascinating," I replied.

"It's a totally new way to make sure the weekly goals you set for yourself actually get done, when you planned to do them. It's a great way to cultivate the self-discipline you need to become a visionary leader when you might not have developed as much of it as you should have. Strategic time blocking will profoundly change your personal effectiveness and revolutionize your productivity. Most leaders suffer from a dreaded disease. Any idea what it's called?"

"Haven't a clue, Julian."

"The disease I am referring to is the disease known only as 'dilution of focus' — and it is one of the most dangerous diseases known to humanity. By diluting their personal focus and trying to be all things to all people, these leaders get nothing done. By diluting their focus and trying to do too many things in too many different directions, they become the victim of their good intentions. Focusing on the worthy and only on the worthy will set your leadership free. It will allow you to do all the things you have wanted to do and dreamed of doing. And strategic time blocking will help you do it."

"Okay, so how do I do it?"

"The first thing you need to do is designate the different days of your week in terms of different areas of focus. It's almost like building a mold according to subject matter for each day and then pouring specific activities into it. If you do so, you will no longer waste your days scrambling to do a hundred different things. Instead, you will focus on a particular area each day and then devote your time to it. For example, Monday could be your day to concentrate only on issues and initiatives that involve your employees. You might label Monday Human Relations Day. Then make sure that any weekly win dealing with that subject gets scheduled on that day. Don't think about sales issues or work on new product development on that day. Stay focused. Next you might designate Tuesday as your Business Development Day. Again, that day will be strictly reserved for activities relating to generating new business. Wednesday might be your day reserved for marketing or finance-related issues. Thursday might be your Open Day, meaning you will be free to deal with any crisis that might come up or to catch up on general administrative issues or just be available for anyone who needs you."

"And what about Friday? What should I designate that day as?"

"You can set it aside for whatever worthy area you would like to focus on. As I've said, you need to be the one to craft and tailor the kind of week that is best suited for you. *Let time be your servant rather than your master.* My suggestion to you, however, is that you reserve Friday as your Renewal Day, the day that you set aside to revitalize your leadership and re-create yourself as an executive. All your weekly wins dealing with this subject are scheduled at this time. You might spend it on strategic thinking and clarifying your future vision for the company. You might dedicate it to preparation and future planning priorities. You could use it to go to a leadership seminar or work with a personal development coach. You might devote it to catching up on all those publications you subscribe to but rarely get a chance to review or to get deep into a hot new management book that will give you some new ideas to catapult GlobalView up to the next level. Or you might use it to brainstorm with your management team. By committing to the time leadership method I am suggesting, you will finally be able to turn all your good intentions into tangible results. Are you beginning to see what strategic time blocking is all about?"

"I am. By applying the concept, my time becomes concentrated on the things that count. And as you and the greatest thinkers have said, concentrating effort and focusing on the worthy is the secret of getting meaningful things done in life. I will no longer get pulled into a million different directions every day and do a hundred different things in a half-hearted way. I will no longer have to leave everything I start unfinished and rush off to put out the next little brush fire. Instead, I'll bring focus to my days by following a weekly cycle of designated focus areas and spending time on the 'worthy' activities that will get us closer to our vision. I can also see that the process will allow me to make time for those all-important 'big-picture' activities, such as flexing my imagination and strategic thinking. I'm really impressed, and I can't wait to try the process out."

"So let me summarize," interjected Julian. "There are five steps to the Time Model for Visionary Leadership. First you must adopt a weekly planning practice and carve out some time, say on Sunday night, to connect to your vision. Your vision will serve as your personal lighthouse, offering guidance and keeping you on the proper course. Step Two involves reviewing your annual victories, those goals you have determined you need to accomplish this year to keep moving forward. Step Three in the process is to come up with a series of weekly wins, or micro goals that you must accomplish during the coming week. Once you have your weekly wins, Step Four requires that you schedule them into your days by applying the technique of strategic time blocking. Every day of the week has a designated area of focus. Schedule each activity into the particular day designated for it and you will ensure that it gets done. It's really pretty simple once you do it for three or four weeks."

"And what about Step Five?"

"Step Five is about what Yogi Raman called 'regular reflection.' *Reflection is the mother of wisdom*, Peter. Never forget that. And having wisdom allows you to make wiser choices, which, in turn, leads to a richer life, both professionally and personally. Every Sunday night, as you plan the coming week, take a few moments to deeply consider the week that you have just lived. Did you do what you planned to do, when you planned to do it? If not, why not? What would you have done differently if you had the chance to spend that week again? Did you truly 'focus on the worthy'? Awareness precedes change, and if you are not aware of the activities you are spending time on, you will never discover that there are ones more deserving of your energy. By reflecting on how you spend your time, you will not only be more effective during the next week, you will also get to know yourself."

"Don't most people know themselves?"

"Not at all. Most people have no real idea of their strengths or their weaknesses. And as a result, they keep on making the same mistakes over and over again throughout their entire lives. By taking the time to reflect on how you are leading and how you are living, you will be able to make those all-important course corrections every week so that you continually grow as a leader — and as a person. Remember, my friend, there's nothing wrong with making a mistake. Mistakes allow us to mature and become wiser. But there *is* something wrong with constantly making the same mistakes. It shows a complete lack of wisdom. Instead, begin to *leverage past errors for future successes. Allow your past to serve you.* That's one of the greatest abilities of visionary leaders. That's also one of the fundamentals of effective living. Regular reflection will ensure that you practice this habit. As Seneca stated: 'As long as you live, keep learning how to live.' "

Darkness now filled the sky, and the only sounds in the air were those of the bullfrogs and crickets. I was really enjoying this evening with Julian. Two old friends, sitting quietly under a starry sky, savoring the pleasures of each other's company and contemplating the larger issues of leadership and life. I wondered why I hadn't thought about these things before. Was I really so busy that I didn't have time to think about the things that truly mattered?

In the weeks since Julian first showed up in the rose garden outside my office, striking changes had taken place within GlobalView. His leadership wisdom had served to give me the wake-up call that I so desperately needed and to show me the path I had to follow if we wanted to reach world-class status as an organization. I had put many of his lessons and philosophies into practice and had trained my entire management team in the rituals for visionary leadership that I had so far been exposed to by Julian. And the changes I had witnessed were nothing short of incredible.

People were buzzing with a new sense of excitement. They felt inspired by the future vision I shared with them and believed they were an integral part of something meaningful. I'd heard some employees saying that, for the first time in years, they were being listened to and their interests were understood. Our new rewards-and-recognition program was a hit as was our first Crazy Day. We had started to come together as a closely knit unit to manage change to our advantage.

After much soul-searching, I myself made some very personal improvements during that period. Through the wisdom Julian had brought into my life, I realized that my role as a leader really was about "freeing people's strengths" and allowing them the freedom to develop themselves as we realized our dreams for GlobalView. I now appreciated, for the first time in my life, the importance of keeping my promises, "listening aggressively," "being consistently compassionate" and becoming "fanatically honest," to use the vocabulary Julian favored. And I started to work hard to manage my temper. Believe me, all my efforts made a world of difference. My wife, Samantha, especially noticed a change in me. Julian was absolutely right when he said that I had to stop blaming others for the troubles of our organization and assume responsibility for its failings. Like he said, "Great leadership precedes great followership."

Morale began to skyrocket, loyalty and commitment returned; people became more productive than they had been in years. They actually started talking about the company as if they were part owners in it, as if they had an investment stake in its success and as if they were in business for themselves. I liked that. Our new suggestion program, which allowed anyone to send management an idea to improve the way we did things at GlobalView via e-mail, led to some amazing innovations that helped us cut costs, enhance effectiveness, serve our customers better, and get closer to our vision for the future. Rest assured, the employees who made those suggestions were amply recognized and rewarded. The leadership wisdom that those sages up in the Himalayas shared with Julian had really worked wonders for us.

"Why do you keep looking at that star, Julian?" I asked as he again stared at the brightest star in the sky. "You said you were going to tell me."

"I will, but the time is not quite right. Soon it will be, for we are coming closer to the end of Yogi Raman's system for visionary leadership. For now, let me just say that that star has been a friend to me. You know I've been through a lot in my life, especially during the past few years with my heart attack and all. Leaving the corporate world was a major act of faith for me and I left a lot behind."

"Like that beautiful Ferrari," I piped in.

"Like that Ferrari," Julian acknowledged. "That star has helped me along the way."

I still had no idea of what Julian was speaking of, but sensing his unwillingness to explain his relationship to that star, I decided not to press the point.

That night, as I climbed into bed and snuggled up to Samantha, my thoughts remained on Julian. Here was a corporate superstar who had come close to the brink of death. He then gave up everything he had and headed off in search of the wisdom that he knew he had always lacked. The man trekked through India and high into the Himalayas until he found the sources he had been searching for. While the Sages of Sivana gave him the secrets of youth and happiness, they also shared with him the rituals of visionary leadership. The transformation he had undergone as a person was nothing short of miraculous. I now realized that the transformation I had begun to undergo as a leader was no less astonishing.

I reached over to the table next to our bed and flipped on the night-light. I stared at the small object that I had carefully placed next to my reading glasses. It was made of wood and had been given to me by Julian just before I left him alone at the military base. It was the next piece of the intricate puzzle that had grown over the time we had been meeting. Once again, I could not make out the lightly colored design on it. And once again, it carried an inscription. It read simply: *Ritual 6: Leader Lead Thyself.*

Chapter 9 Knowledge Summary • Julian's Wisdom in a Nutshell

The Ritual

Focus
on the
Worthy™

The Essence

The Ritual of Personal Effectiveness

The Wisdom

- The secret of personal effectiveness is concentration of purpose
- The art of getting things done lies in knowing what things need to remain undone
- If you do not lead your time, it will lead you
- If your priorities do not get scheduled into your planner, other peoples' priorities will get scheduled into your planner

The Practices

- The Time Model for Visionary Leadership™
- Strategic Time Blocking™

Quotable Quote

Never forget the importance of each and every one of your days. As you live your days, so you live your life. Do not waste even one of them. The past is history and the future is but a figment. This day, the present, is really all you have.

The Monk Who Sold His Ferrari

RITUAL 6

❦

Leader Lead Thyself

CHAPTER TEN

The Ritual of Self-Leadership

There is nothing noble in being superior to others.
True nobility lies in being superior to your former self.

Ancient Indian proverb

MOUNT PERCIVAL IS THE TALLEST PEAK in this part of the country. Mountaineers and adventurers come from far and wide to scale its north face, apparently one of the most treacherous of all of the climbs in our locale. A few years ago, the son of one of my colleagues lost his life on a summit attempt. He and the seven members of his team had been found frozen to death about two hundred feet from the top. For the life of me, I could not figure out why Julian wanted me to meet him here.

As I drove my four-wheel drive up the winding highway that led to an area near the base of the mountain frequented by tourists and hikers, I realized I had come to rely on Julian's regular coaching sessions. Every single one of our meetings had not only been rich with leadership wisdom and powerful lessons on organizational transformation, they had also been mini-adventures that moved me out of my "region of security," to borrow from Julian's language, and into new pathways of thought and action. I sensed that he would not remain in one place for a very long time since I knew he was deeply committed to spreading the philosophy of the sages throughout our part of the world. And I knew that when he left, I would miss him.

As I drove up to the base area, crowded with people from all across the world on this fine day, I spotted Julian. Unlike the last time, today he had on his traditional ruby red monk's robe and his well-worn sandals. As usual, his face radiated vitality and good health. And as on each of the previous occasions, it carried a smile. It was still a little hard for me to believe that this youthful-looking man was actually Julian Mantle, the once hard-drinking, fast-living corporate player who had collapsed from a massive heart attack in the middle of a packed courtroom.

"Greetings, Peter!" Julian said with his usual degree of enthusiasm. "It's quite a day up here on the mountain," he added, taking a whiff of fresh air deep into his lungs. "Kind of makes me feel as if I was back in the Himalayas with Yogi Raman and the rest of my wise teachers."

"Do you miss their company?"

"Terribly. They were the kindest, most giving men and women I have ever known. They treated me like I was a part of their small family, and I felt like they were a part of mine. Those days, up in that natural oasis of beauty, peace and knowledge were truly the best of my life. Having said that, I made a promise to them, and I plan to keep it. I have a duty to perform and will dedicate the rest of my days to spreading their ideas about leadership in business and in life, making sure that their timeless message is heard by all those who need to hear it."

"Mind if I ask another question?"

"Not at all," Julian replied as we walked to the lodge to purchase a ticket up the mountain by cable car.

"Why are we going up there?" I asked as I strained my neck to look up at the summit.

"Because there is another leadership lesson I wish to share with you. And that is the perfect place for me to share it."

As we rode up the mountain, neither of us said a word. The beauty of the scenery was simply breathtaking, something to be taken in fully — and silently. With the feeling of joy that came over me through this connection to the gifts of nature, I wondered why I did not leave that oak-paneled office of mine more often to get outdoors and enjoy the simple pleasures of life. At least, I could bring Samantha and the kids up here on weekends. I really needed to spend more time with them. And I knew that such an outing would bring a greater sense of perspective to my days along with energy to my weeks.

After about half an hour of steady climbing, the cable car stopped abruptly and a voice on the public address system asked us to "de-car," a term I had never heard before and prayed I wouldn't again. Julian, obviously familiar with the place, led me along a snow-covered walkway lined on both sides with thick strands of rope. I silently followed my friend, placing my full trust in this man, who I had learned had my best interests in mind. Finally we arrived at our destination. And it was like nothing I had ever seen.

The ridge we were standing on looked out across the entire region as well as over other smaller mountains, which struggled to push through the billowy clouds in the otherwise clear blue sky. I truly wished Samantha and the kids were there with me. This sight would have amazed them. I felt deeply peaceful in this heavenly place and shared this sentiment with my youthful companion.

"I know what you mean, my friend. I know what you mean." After a few minutes of soaking in the view, Julian began his lesson.

"Ritual 6 is an extremely important one, Peter, one that visionary leaders practice on a daily basis. If they fail to do so, even for a few days, their vision is diminished and much of their effectiveness is lost."

"Exactly what does Leader Lead Thyself mean?" I asked as I pulled the sixth piece of the puzzle from the light ski jacket I had put on for the occasion and glanced more closely at it.

"Ritual 6 is the ritual of self-leadership. Sadly, self-leadership is the discipline most neglected by leaders in this part of the world. And yet, it is the foundation from which all other success in business and in life springs."

"Is self-leadership the same as self-improvement?"

"It's about so much more than that. Sir Edmund Hillary, who as you know was the first person to reach the summit of Mount Everest, said it best when he observed: 'It is not the mountain we conquer but ourselves.' That's really the essence of self-leadership — it's about conquering and mastering yourself."

"Interesting."

"Most leaders believe that effectiveness and excellence come from external factors like an efficient work force or application of the latest technology. The truth of the matter, as visionary leaders have known over the centuries, is that success is an inside job. Excellence begins within. Market leadership begins with self-leadership."

After inhaling another deep breath of the crisp mountain air, Julian continued. "You see, Peter, how can you lead an organization if you've never learned how to lead yourself? How can you coach a team if you've never mastered the art of self-coaching? And how can you expect to manage others if you've never refined the skill of managing yourself?"

"My dad used to say that you can't do good if you don't feel good."

"Precisely. And Goethe made the point in a similar way when he noted that 'before you can do something you must *be* something.' You cannot be the inspirational leader you hope to be if you wake up every morning feeling miserable and depressed. You cannot guide your people forward to victory if you are being kept behind by a lack of energy. You will not be able to capture their hearts and energize their minds if you are still yelling and screaming at them all day. Remember, before you can like another person, you must like yourself. *Success on the outside begins within.*

"It's like that old story my favorite professor told me when I was in law school," Julian added. "One night a father was relaxing with his newspaper after a long day at the office. His son, who wanted to play, kept on pestering him. Finally, fed up, the father ripped out a picture of the globe that was in the paper and tore it into many tiny pieces. 'Here, son, go ahead and try to put this back together,' he said, hoping this would keep the little boy busy long enough for him to finish reading his paper. To his amazement, his son returned after only one minute with the globe perfectly reassembled. When the startled father asked how he achieved this feat, the child smiled gently and replied, 'Dad, on the other side of the globe there was a picture of a person, and once I got the person together, the world was okay.' "

"So the lesson is that success on the outside really does begin within. It all starts by getting myself together. And once I do, my own world will be okay, correct?"

"Yes, Peter, that's it exactly."

"Are you suggesting that I make personal mastery one of my major goals?"

"Make it a vow."

"What's the difference?"

"A goal is something you aim to do, a positive intention that you plan to achieve sometime in the future. I discovered from the sages that a vow is something much deeper than that. Making a vow means you are committed, from the very core of your character, to keeping the promise you have made. Failure is simply not an option. By making a vow, you simply refuse to lose."

"Self-leadership is really that important?"

"Definitely. All the great thinkers have known of this truth. Seneca said, 'To master one's self is the greatest mastery,' while Confucius noted that 'good people strengthen themselves ceaselessly.' 'Man is made and unmade by himself,' discovered James Allen, while the sixth-century Chinese military leader Sun Tzu said, 'To secure ourselves against defeat lies in our own hands.' Even the modern leadership philosopher Peter Drucker observed that 'self-development of the effective executive is central to the development of the organization, whether it be a business, a government agency, a research laboratory, a hospital or a military service. It is the way toward performance of the organization.'

"You see, my friend, one of the most enduring of all the ancient laws of humanity is that *we see the world not as it is, but as we are.* By improving, refining, and defining who we are, we see the world from the highest, most enlightened perspective. By mastering ourselves, we see the world and all its limitless opportunities and potential from the top of the mountain rather than from the bottom. Commit yourself to excellence. Raise the personal standards you have set for yourself. Strive to do everything spectacularly well. *Remember that when you settle for mediocrity in the small things, you will also begin to settle for mediocrity in the big things. And anything less than a conscious commitment to peak personal performance is an unconscious commitment to weak personal performance.*

As I absorbed this profound piece of leadership wisdom, I gazed off into the horizon. I had never taken the time to think about self-improvement. I had often seen other executives reading personal development books, such as *As a Man Thinketh, University of Success, Think and Grow Rich, Psycho-Cybernetics* and *MegaLiving,* on my frequent airline flights and thought silently, *There but for the grace of God go I,* assuming that these were poor souls suffering a professional or a personal crisis. I now realized that while those who could effectively manage others were wise, those who had mastered themselves were enlightened. The most important thing any leader could do to improve his organization was to first improve himself. My dad was right. You can't do good if you don't feel good. It is impossible to do great things if you are not thinking great thoughts. I had to make a "vow," as Julian suggested, to get serious about the development of my self so I could achieve all the things I wanted to achieve. I had to Focus on the Worthy and make the time to lift my inner life to a whole new level of effectiveness.

"Now do you see why I brought you up to the top of this mountain? To gain leadership over others, you must gain true leadership over yourself," Julian said. "You must climb your own mountains and rise to the top, conquering yourself in the process. You must stop making excuses for why things have gone wrong and assume some responsibility for a change. Visionary leaders are alibi-free."

"What do you mean by alibi-free?" I queried.

"As a litigation lawyer, I had the opportunity to cross-examine thousands of witnesses over the course of my career. No matter how guilty they were, they all did the same thing. They all came up with an excuse that shifted the blame to someone else. Not once could they clearly and simply admit, 'It was all my fault. I was wrong. And I am truly sorry.' "

"They all had alibis."

"Right. But visionary leaders are the masters of themselves, as well as of their destinies. They know that if there is a problem with morale in the company, there is a problem with their leadership. They understand that if their relationships are lacking in depth and warmth, there must be some lack within themselves. They know that if their levels of personal achievement are less than outstanding, the thoughts they are having and the actions they are taking must be less than superb. That's why I say that visionary leaders are alibi-free. They have the power of character to realize that they ultimately control their futures and that their outer lives are shaped by their inner ones.

"And just like scaling any great mountain," added Julian enthusiastically, "the higher you climb within yourself, the more you will see. The more you come to know who and what you really are as a person, performer and as a leader, the more value you will be able to contribute to the world around you. The saddest thing I know of is a human being who has no sense of self, no idea of what she could achieve in her life if only she had the courage to liberate her full potential through the discipline of self-mastery. Too many people live far below their potential. It's like Wordsworth once wrote: 'The world is too much with us; late and soon,/ Getting and spending, we lay waste our powers:/ Little we see in nature that is ours;/ We have given our hearts away, a sordid boon!' The point I'm really trying to make can be made very simply: *Leadership in your world begins with leadership of your life.*"

Julian then walked over to a long wooden bench that rested along the ridge and sat down. Closing his eyes and again deeply breathing in the cool, clean air of this spectacular mountain hideaway, he paused before continuing his passionate discourse on the value of self-leadership.

"You know, Peter, I really love this place. Since I've returned from the Himalayas, I've probably been up here fifty times. It really keeps my head clear. Life with the sages was so serene and peaceful. While they were enormously productive people, their achievement was of a graceful sort. Now that I'm back, I have to admit that I must constantly try not to get swept up in the frenetic pace that dogs our society."

"I feel the same way," I replied. "I mean the pace that I keep at the office is crazy. I'm like a wild man most days. Did you know that my executive assistant, Arielle, has already organized my appointment schedule for the next thirteen months? The number of people I have to see and the amount of work I have to do is absolutely unbelievable. Though the Time Model for Visionary Leadership that you shared with me is beginning to free me to Focus on the Worthy, I still feel the stress."

"Which brings me nicely to the first of the 5 Ancient Disciplines for Self-Leadership. These disciplines are formulations of the timeless wisdom that Yogi Raman gave me for personal mastery. Best practices for human excellence and inner leadership, if you will. Yogi Raman saw that I was in pretty bad shape when I arrived in the Himalayas, still recovering from my heart attack. So he offered me a series of philosophies and techniques to get my internal world back into shape. Let me simply say that the changes that followed when I applied these strategies were profound. The sense of tranquility that I had lost as a corporate superstar returned. I was able to conquer the worry habit that had plagued me for so long. My energy levels soared. I began to feel the way I had as an idealistic kid at Harvard Law School. And I knocked many years off the way I looked."

"No kidding," I observed with a smile. "I thought you were some kid when I saw you standing in my rose garden that day. Your transformation is astonishing. I'd love to hear how you did it. What's the First Discipline for Self-Leadership?"

"It's the Discipline of Personal Renewal. All visionary leaders regularly renew themselves. They make time to revitalize their bodies and energize their spirits. You see, in these information-crazed times that we live in, leaders and managers are being driven to do more with less, to work smarter, faster and harder. This frenetic pace that you are required to maintain just to keep up with the competition takes its toll on the way you think, feel and perform. But the thing you need to remember is that it's not really the stress that diminishes your effectiveness and leaves you feeling utterly exhausted at the end of the day."

"It's not?"

"No. What really does the damage is the failure of most leaders and managers to gain some *relief* from the inevitable stresses they face. As I told you earlier, some anxiety is always associated with change and change is the dominant force in business today. To thrive in this new economy, you have to work harder and aim higher. But virtues can become vices when practiced to excess, and overwork needs to be balanced with downtime. The best way to do this is to get regular relief through self-renewal activities. As the Chinese philosopher Lao Tzu said, 'All action begins in rest. That is the ultimate truth.' This will make you stress-hardy and allow you to maintain high levels of stamina and creativity for longer periods of time. I suggest you make a weekly sabbatical a top priority."

"What's a weekly sabbatical?"

"In the old days, people were required to observe a day of rest at the end of each working week. This day, known as the Sabbath, was used to relax, connect with family, enjoy personal hobbies or pursue spiritual activities. As a result, workers would begin the new week full of energy, zeal, and conviction, ready to face the challenges their jobs would inevitably provide. Sadly, this tradition has been passed over, for most people and hard-driving executives believe that nonstop work routines are the only way to get to the top. It is only when they are afflicted with ulcers, migraines, and early heart attacks that they wake up and begin to change the way they work and live. Unfortunately, by then it is sometimes too late. Believe me, my friend, I'm speaking from personal experience.

"So what I'm suggesting," continued Julian, "is that you designate a period every single week for some serious personal renewal. Time spent recharging your batteries is never a waste but a necessary aspect of any peak performance routine. Recreation is about re-creation. Time spent on genuine recreation makes you stronger, smarter and a better leader. Abe Lincoln captured the essence of what I am saying when he remarked, 'If I had eight hours to chop down a tree, I'd spend six hours sharpening my axe.' "

"So what you are saying is that working the way I do, without ever taking a vacation or even a regular day off to unwind, is the same as driving my BMW full-out, day after day without ever taking the time for a pit stop."

"Right. *Failing to devote time to the discipline of self-renewal is like saying you are so busy driving that you don't have time to stop for gas.* Not the smartest way to think, is it?"

"I agree. But how can I make time for myself?"

"I've already given you the secret."

"Really?"

"Use the Time Model for Visionary Leadership and the technique of strategic time blocking that I shared with you when we were at the military base. During your Sunday night planning practice, which I know you have begun to ritualize, block out a period over the coming week for recreation, relaxation, and the renewal that you need to perform at your best. Make sure that at least one of your weekly wins revolves around quiet time. And plan to invest at least one hour on your weekly sabbatical. It will return huge dividends to you over the long run, especially when it comes to effective thinking and problem solving in your work as a leader."

"Seriously?"

"Sure, Descartes made many of his most important intellectual discoveries while relaxing in bed, and Newton formulated the laws of gravity while meditating under an apple tree. Archimedes stumbled upon the laws of hydrostatics while soaking in a hot bath and Mozart composed one of his most famous pieces over a game of billiards. Even the sewing machine came about through an act of renewal."

"Really?"

"Elias Howe, a Massachusetts instrument maker, was deep in sleep when he had a bizarre dream. In it, he was being chased by a man carrying a long spear with a small hole at the end of it. This served as the inspiration for his invention that later became known to the world as the sewing machine. Are you beginning to see how much the world would have missed had these visionaries not understood the power of self-renewal?"

"I am, Julian. I am," I replied as I pondered this lesson. "Can you give me a sense of what kinds of things I should be doing during my weekly sabbatical?"

"The best suggestion I have is to go for a walk in natural surroundings and discover the power of solitude. According to Native American tradition, a human being is like a house with three rooms — your mind, your body and your spirit. To live fully, you must fill these rooms daily with sunlight and fresh air. In our time-starved, fast-paced world, we have forgotten the importance of time spent alone, in silent contemplation. And yet, such reflection is also the surest route to wisdom, both in your leadership and within your life. Reflection and introspection allow you to analyze why you do what you do and how to make continual improvements. The practice of quiet contemplation will enrich your judgment and allow you to begin to understand not just *what* is happening around you at the office but *why* it is happening. It will allow you to grow more aware of the consequences of each of your choices and, therefore, improve your decision-making abilities. Essentially, making the time for regular reflection will allow you to learn from living. All of humanity's great advances, whether technological or artistic, came, not from frenzied activity but from the deep reflection and introspection that quiet time brings. And connecting to nature will soothe your frazzled nerves and bring a greater sense of balance into your life."

"Any other ideas for my weekly sabbatical?"

"How about planning to spend an hour in a used bookstore, just flipping through great books and enjoying some time alone. Why not go for a massage or watch the sun rise early on Sunday morning. Why not take one of those wonderful kids you have out on a long hike or simply spend a Saturday afternoon by the sea, watching the waves break against a rocky shore. Don't be so busy chasing the big things in life that you neglect life's simple pleasures. *Don't be so busy striving to make a living that you forget how to live a life."*

I was stunned by the phrase that Julian had just uttered. He was absolutely right. My chaotic, out-of-control lifestyle was leading me to disaster. Sure, a solid work ethic was an essential element of success. Even Julian would agree with that truth. But the strain I had been under as GlobalView's market share and morale slipped had started to affect my health. I realized I was working compulsively and was more concerned about the time I spent in the office than the quality of the results I was producing. I always felt tired, I was even more irritable than usual and I was rarely able to get a good night's sleep. By living my life like it was some kind of an Olympic sprint, never taking the time to read a good book over lunch or watch the sun set on a weekend, I was missing out on the best life had to offer. I vowed I would change. My employees deserved a calmer leader. My wife deserved a better husband. My kids deserved a better father. And I deserved a lot more peace.

"What's the Second Discipline for Self-Leadership?" I asked, interrupting my own thoughts.

"It's the Discipline of Abundant Knowledge. Yogi Raman believed that applied knowledge is perhaps the greatest source of power and every leader was duty-bound to reserve at least thirty

minutes a day to read. Books will keep you connected to the fundamental leadership principles that all too often get forgotten in the
crush of daily activities. Thirty minutes of concentrated reading
every single day of the week will make a profound difference in
your life. Every answer to every problem you have ever faced lies
in print. Whether you want to be a better leader, thinker, father, or
golfer, a book surely exists that will rocket you to your goal. All the
mistakes that you will ever make in your life have already been
made by those who walked the earth before you. Do you really
think that the challenges you face are unique to you?"

"No."

"Then learn from the experience and wisdom of those who
have gone before you. Just think about it: books allow you to look
deeply into the minds of the greatest men and women who have
ever lived. By investing the few hours that it takes to read the
autobiography of Gandhi or the biography of Churchill, you will
learn the leadership lessons that it took them decades to discover.
You will come to understand the principles they followed as well as
the solutions they discovered to many of the most common leadership problems. By reading from books on executive effectiveness and personal mastery, you will find time-honored ways to get
more done in less time. And by reading the great works of philosophy and consistently exposing your mind to the great thinkers,
you will come to understand the ageless laws of nature and
humanity. As Yogi Raman once told me, '*Stop wishing for fewer
problems and start searching for greater wisdom.*' "

"Wow. What a statement!"

"What I'm really telling you to do by suggesting that you read
for thirty minutes a day is to apply the Principle of Association."

"Which says?"

"It says that the type of leader and the kind of person you will be five years from now will result from two primary influences: the books you read and the people you associate with. Start spending some of your day with the greatest people who ever lived by spending some time with the books they have written. How would you like to have Napoleon Hill or Dale Carnegie as your personal success coaches, just waiting for you to give them the word? How would you like to have Ben Franklin, Thomas Edison, or Alexander Graham Bell mentoring you on the fundamentals of creative thinking and innovation? How would you like to have Abe Lincoln sitting on your bedside table, always available to school you on leadership strategy or Mother Teresa waiting in your den just waiting to teach you the value of patience and compassion in all that you do? That's the power of print. All of the wisdom of these enlightened humans lies within the pages of their books. Regularly associating with them allows you to rise to their level of thought."

"Much like an intermediate tennis player always plays a better game when she plays an expert."

"Excellent analogy. Remember, it's not just what you get out of books that makes the difference — it's what books bring out of you. I also suggest you make use of some of the more modern forms of knowledge and intelligence that are waiting for you to call them into action."

"Like what?"

"Like audiocassette programs. Did you know that if you commute thirty minutes each way every day, after one year this time will have amounted to six weeks of eight-hour days?"

"I had no idea I spent that much time in the car. That's a month and a half that I'm spending on the road every year. Unbelievable."

"With a number like that, you really should be listening to

educational and motivational tapes in your car on the way to work and then again on your way home. Your employees will notice a big difference every morning and your family a big difference every night. Why not take control of the information that you feed your mind while you commute and ensure that it is the kind that will add value to your life? Set the goal of listening to at least one new audio-book or cassette program per week. You can also practice the Discipline of Abundant Knowledge by going to personal development seminars. And encourage your people to do the same. Let the power of self-leadership spread through your entire organization and transform the culture into one of top performance."

"What about the Internet?"

"I hear that's another superb method to tap into every possible type of information you could ever hope for to improve both your business and your life. Like I said earlier, commit to becoming a lifelong student. *Learning no longer ends the minute you pass your last exam. It must continue until you take your last breath.*"

"So what's the next discipline I can follow to cultivate self-leadership? I'm really getting excited about all you are telling me and can't wait to put it into practice. I used to read so much more than I do now. I know spending time with great books will bring a greater sense of perspective, not to mention sanity, back into my life. I must admit, I'd hate to leave this world without having read the great works of wisdom and literature."

"Nice point," offered Julian. "The Third Discipline for Self-Leadership is the Discipline of Physicality, as Yogi Raman called it. It simply involves making sure that you respect the timeless truth that says, *as you care for your body, so you care for your mind.* Visionary leaders are high-performance leaders. And high-performance leaders need vigor, energy and drive, the kind that comes through being in prime physical condition. You must have the wisdom to exercise regularly and eat to win. There are 168 hours in a week. Surely you can find a few to swim, stretch, or run."

"You know, I've been meaning to get back into shape for quite some time. In college I was quite a track star."

"I had no idea."

"I used to love working out in the good old days. I know that if I just took twenty or thirty minutes to go for a swim at lunch, it would make a big difference in the way I feel, act, and think. I just finished reading Nelson Mandela's autobiography."

"A visionary leader if there ever was one."

"I agree. Do you know what he did for exercise?"

"I know he used to rise at dawn and walk."

"That was in his later years. But in his early days, to stay in peak physical condition, he used to box. He absolutely loved the sport and said that the activity renewed him completely. 'It was a way of losing myself in something that was not the struggle,' he wrote. 'After an evening's workout, I would wake up the next morning feeling strong and refreshed, ready to take up the fight again.' "

"Like I said, visionary leaders know that when you care for your body, you also care for your mind. And get this, according to a study at my alma mater involving 17,000 Harvard alumni, it was found that every hour you exercise adds another three hours to your life. Now, that's an excellent return on investment. So what are you waiting for? Now is the time to get into peak condition. It will add so much to the quality of both your professional and personal life. It will make you feel wonderful and give you the energy to do all the meaningful things you want to do. It will even enhance the clarity of your thoughts. And like the sages said, *The person who doesn't make time for exercise must eventually make time for illness.*"

"Any suggestions as to the best type of exercise?"

"It's really up to you. Try to find a sport or activity that is fun. Myself, I love the simple discipline of walking. It's convenient, healthy and enjoyable. Many of the world's most productive and creative people have been recreational walkers. When Charles Dickens suffered from writer's block, he would walk the streets of London late at night hoping to rekindle his creative fire. Day after day he would stroll and study the sights. During his outings, he observed many young children working for little or no pay, a circumstance that deeply troubled him. His desire to shed light on this problem sparked his creativity, leading him to write his most famous work, *A Christmas Carol.*

"Fascinating."

"Swiss designer George de Mestral came up with the idea for Velcro after taking long walks in the mountains. He noticed that his dog's fur was covered by burdock burrs after these jaunts. When he looked at these closely under a microscope, he noticed they were made up of hundreds of tiny hooks that had stuck to the fur. He realized that these would be far more effective than zippers and ultimately produced the first Velcro fastener. What I'm getting at is that walking is a superb way to renew and revitalize your mind as well as your body. All the great thinkers knew this. Confucius, Aristotle, and Socrates, for example, all implored their disciples to walk regularly to maintain perfect health. As Yogi Raman used to say with a smile, 'I have two doctors I always keep with me. My right leg and my left one.' "

"You also suggested that I eat to win. What do you mean by that?"

"The sages understood that the quality of the food you ingest affects the quality of your thoughts. And in this information age, we all know that rich ideas are the foundation of success. We have entered a knowledge economy where intellectual capital carries the highest value in the marketplace. And if you agree that the food you eat affects the way you think, eating well is not just sound health practice. It makes good business sense."

"Who would have thought that the junk food I wolf down every lunch hour was affecting our bottom line?"

"Of course, it does. You have a steak and fries for lunch and you feel exhausted, right?"

"True."

"So your choice of food has diminished both your creativity and your productivity. Consider the effect that kind of lunch has on your bottom line when it is consumed not just by you but by many others in the organization. That's why I say eat to win. Adopt a peak performance diet. Eat more vegetables and fruits. Drink more water. Reduce the quantities of food that you ingest since most of us eat far more than we need to. Get serious about your health. It will even help you with that sleep problem you've been complaining about. Which brings me to the Fourth Discipline for Self-Leadership, the Discipline of Early Awakening."

"I have a feeling I'm not going to like this one."

"Getting up early is a common practice that runs through the lives of history's greatest people. Visionary leaders in the fields of business, arts, the military, and the sciences have understood that if you don't control the day, it will control you. You must have the courage to win the battle of the bed and rise before most others do. Enjoy the exceptional tranquility that the day's earliest hours brings and bask in the splendor of the morning, before the crush of daily events clamors for your mind's attention. The sages believed that *as you start your day, so you live your day.* They believed that the first thirty minutes after awakening set the tone for the entire day so they had to be special ones.

"By getting up early, you become the master of your time rather than it mastering you. Thomas Edison, whose industrious work habits allowed him to record over 1,093 inventions in his lifetime, said that 'sleep is like a drug. Take too much at a time and it makes you dopey. You lose time, vitality and opportunities.' Ben Franklin believed that there would be more than enough time to sleep when we were in our graves."

"Sounds a little extreme, Julian. I mean, don't we all need sleep?"

"Yes, we do. The problem is that most people sleep far more than they need to. They have developed a habit of oversleeping and then claim that their bodies can't do without it. Do you want to hear the real reason that most people don't get up early?"

"Sure."

"Most people don't get up early because they wouldn't know what to do with their time if they did. They lack a passionate purpose that fuels and energizes their lives. And so they sleep. That's why I told you earlier that purpose is one of the greatest motivators known to humankind and that, as a visionary leader, you must link your people's work to a compelling cause that satisfies their human hunger to contribute and make a difference to others' lives. People who lack energy often lack a dynamic future vision that impels them forward and excites their spirits. Gandhi slept only four hours a night. His personal mission to free his people from the shackles of servitude was enough fuel to drive him forward. Mandela was an early riser as were many of the wealthiest industrialists who founded this great nation. Always remember that there is a close connection between your energy levels and your purpose."

"Fascinating. So when I become truly committed to my compelling cause, I will have more energy and not feel so tired all the time?"

"Right. And you will actually feel like rising early because you are excited about where you are going and the good work that you are doing. Which brings me to the Fifth and Final Discipline for Self-Leadership — the Discipline of the Deathbed Mentality."

"Sounds morbid."

"Funny you should think that, because this practice is all about life. According to ancient legend, there was once a maharaja in India who began his day by following a peculiar personal rite. Every morning, just after he arose, he would celebrate his own funeral, complete with flowers and music, all the while chanting, 'I have lived fully. I have lived fully.' "

"Bizarre."

"That's what I thought when I first heard about it. But then I realized that the maharaja was on to something. You see, he had found his own way to do what every single one of us needs to do every morning after we wake up."

"Which is?" I asked, still having no idea what the maharaja's strange ritual was designed to accomplish.

"Connect with our mortality. Most of us live every day as if we had all the time in the world. We will explore that new opportunity *next* week. We will learn that new skill *next* month. We will start to improve our health or spend more time with our kids *next* year. But right now, we tell ourselves that there are so many things on our plates that demand our immediate attention that we couldn't possibly have time for anything else."

"I'm still not sure I understand exactly what the maharaja was doing," I admitted.

"By celebrating his funeral, he was reminding himself that life is short. He was connecting with the fact that each day could be his last. And by doing so, he brought a sense of urgency, drive, and passion to his days that the vast majority of leaders and managers lack. By connecting to his own mortality, he ensured that he lived life fully and didn't put off doing the important things. Every single day became a work of art, his tiny tribute to the gift of living. I'm sure you'll agree, Peter, that most of us live as if we had all the time in the world. We worry about trifling matters and focus on petty things. We brood about past failures and fret over future events. We rush through life as if it were a dress rehearsal. And then, on our deathbeds, our hearts fill with regret when we reflect on all the initiatives we did not pursue, on all the relationships we did not build, on all the adventures we did not explore and on all the sunrises that we slept through. I've always found it ironic that people say they would give anything for a little more time in their days and yet they waste the precious time they already have."

"How true. I know exactly what you mean, Julian. I look at my kids and can't believe how quickly time is passing. Christopher will soon be eleven and Elliot fourteen. Yet it seems that it was just yesterday that I was singing them to sleep in their nursery. I've really missed out on a lot of precious moments with those wonderful kids. And there are so many other things I've wanted to do but never got around to doing. Time seems to slip away so quickly. Life is really leaving me behind."

"It's like I said earlier, Peter, either you act on life or life will act on you. But in either case, life waits for nobody. Stop spending so much time thinking about the success of others and start focusing on your own vision for the future. Have the courage to understand that every minute spent thinking about someone else's victories is a minute taken away from the fulfillment of your own. Stop putting off your hopes and dreams to another day. Stop putting off becoming the kind of leader you know in your heart you can be. Now is the time to make things happen. Now is the time to take some risks in your leadership. Now is the time to test those new strategies you have been thinking of testing. Now is the time to show your people how much you value them. Now is the time to really love your family and commit to your community. Do all those things you have always wanted to do, whether that means learning how to play the saxophone or mastering that golf game of yours. Climb the mountain of life and see what life looks like from the summit. You will see things others cannot see. Be like that maharaja. Live every day as if it were your last. Otherwise you will die with the best you had to give still within you."

Julian then reached into his robe and pulled out an unexpected gift. It was a parchment scroll that appeared old and wrinkled through the ravages of time. It had been rolled up like a college degree and carefully tied with a homemade bow.

"Here, my friend. I've been meaning to give you this for some time now. Our friendship has always meant a lot to me, even if I didn't always have the courtesy to show it. I truly want you to lead the kind of joyful and meaningful life I feel is everybody's birthright. This small token will help you on your leadership journey and remind you of a great truth. It contains one of the best definitions of the purpose of life that I have ever read. My hope is that it will be as helpful to your personal growth as it has been to mine."

I immediately untied the bow and studied the words that had been lovingly etched on the scroll. They were elegant in their simplicity and timeless in their leadership wisdom. They were the words of the great philosopher Emerson and they spoke volumes about what true success was all about. They read:

> *To laugh often and love much; to win the respect of intelligent persons and the affection of children; to earn the approbation of honest critics; to appreciate beauty; to give of one's self, to leave the world a bit better, whether by a healthy child, a garden patch or a redeemed social condition; to have played and laughed with enthusiasm and sung with exultation; to know even one life has breathed easier because you have lived — that is to have succeeded.*

As we boarded the cable car to return to the base of the mountain, I reflected on the lessons that Julian had shared with me for self-leadership. I knew that the Disciplines of Personal Renewal, Abundant Knowledge, Physicality, Early Awakening, and Deathbed Thinking would make a big difference in the way I lived. There was absolutely no doubt in my mind about that. Rather than just getting *through* life, now I had a sense of how to start getting *from* life.

On that magical day, moving slowly down that grand mountain while taking in the splendors of nature with a friend who had found enlightenment, I finally realized that success really was an "inside job" and that *visionary leadership ultimately began with inner leadership.* I finally realized this was a great time to be alive and that I now had to live with a greater sense of commitment. And I became aware that I would never truly be able to liberate the talents of others until I first realized the potential within myself.

The Ritual

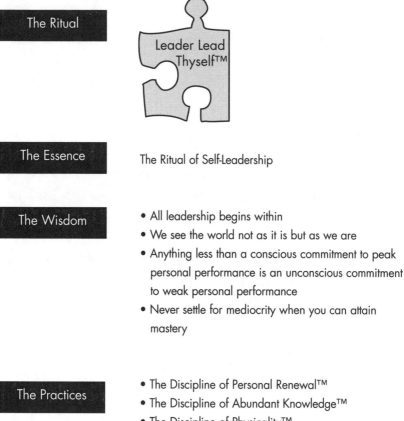

Leader Lead Thyself™

The Essence

The Ritual of Self-Leadership

The Wisdom

- All leadership begins within
- We see the world not as it is but as we are
- Anything less than a conscious commitment to peak personal performance is an unconscious commitment to weak personal performance
- Never settle for mediocrity when you can attain mastery

The Practices

- The Discipline of Personal Renewal™
- The Discipline of Abundant Knowledge™
- The Discipline of Physicality™
- The Discipline of Early Awakening™
- The Discipline of The Deathbed Mentality™

Do not be so busy striving that you miss out on living.

Quotable Quote

The Monk Who Sold His Ferrari

RITUAL 7

⚜

See What All See,
Think What None Think

The Ritual of Creativity and Innovation

Read every day something no one else is reading.
Think every day something no one else is thinking.
It is bad for the mind to be always part of unanimity.

Christopher Morley

"OUR MEETING WILL BE a very short one," Julian had remarked before we parted ways at the mountain's base.

"Why?" I had asked, clearly disappointed.

"Because I'm in the midst of preparing to move. My work with you is almost complete. You have eagerly embraced the leadership philosophy that I have shared and have been a first-rate student. I have no doubt that GlobalView will quickly soar to world-class status and prosper as never before under your visionary leadership. More important, you have now discovered how to lead yourself as well as make GlobalView a place where your people's natural gifts can be freed and their highest hopes fulfilled. Keep serving your people well by liberating their talents and reminding them of the compelling cause they are working toward. They will serve you well in return."

"Where are you going?"

"There is another person who is in desperate need of the wisdom I have discovered, and therefore it is my duty to go."

"Are you going to leave that little hut you made in the forest? It looked like you had everything you needed there."

"Let's just say I've got to leave for a while. But, who knows, you just might see me standing in your rose garden in a few months from now," Julian had said with a wink.

Now, driving to meet with Julian, the thought that I would not see him in the future made me feel very sad. He had always been a friend, but I now saw him in a very special light. No one had had such an influence on me, not even my dad. There were so many other leaders in trouble that Julian could have visited, but he came to me first. If there was one quality he had always possessed in abundance it was loyalty. I was his friend, so he decided to help me.

His coaching sessions were like nothing I had ever experienced before in my life. Within them, Julian had pushed me to explore new pathways of thought and evaluate why I did what I did. He forced me to dig deep and reflect on who I was, not only as a leader, but as a person. He had shared pearls of leadership wisdom with me during those times that I had never heard from any other source, wisdom that had left me feeling motivated, inspired, and fulfilled. I prayed that our paths would soon cross again after he left for his new destination. I needed a friend and mentor like this in my life, as we all do. And I wanted to have the opportunity to do something for him in return.

As I veered off a main road and into a leafy area that was home to middle-class families with station wagons and minivans in their driveways, I spotted my destination. Centennial Elementary School is known far and wide as one of the finest educational institutions in the country, a facility that produces an extraordinary number of gifted kids. Educators come from far and wide to study the innovative teaching methods employed by the dedicated teachers who are lucky enough to be selected as staff members. And although the students are all below the age of ten, they are constantly encouraged to expand their abilities and dream of great futures. This is the kind of school every parent hopes his or her children will have the privilege to attend.

Julian had already arrived and was in the center of the playground, chatting with Mrs. Maples, the famed principal who frequently appeared in the national media to air her views on the current state of education, including her opinion that schools had to place a greater emphasis on the development of character. Although he was wearing his robe and sandals, she didn't seem to mind. As a matter of fact, she appeared to know him and smiled as he spoke.

"Hi, Peter!" Julian shouted enthusiastically as I set foot into the playground, which had just started to fill with noisy little children enjoying their mid-morning recess. "I'd like you to meet a very dear friend of mine, Mildred Maples."

"It's a pleasure to meet you, Mildred," I said, extending my hand. "I've seen you many times on television."

"Nice to meet you too, Peter. I've heard a lot about you as well. Read about you and your company in the papers. You've been very successful."

"That was awhile ago, I'm sorry to admit. We encountered some growing pains along the way that led us into serious difficulties. Having said that, Julian here has really helped me turn things around. It's like I'm running a brand-new company. I hope you don't mind my saying so, but I think you'll be hearing a lot about us again."

"I'll look forward to it," Mrs. Maples replied courteously.

"Mind if I ask you two how you know each other?"

They both started to giggle. "Mildred's husband owns the local Ferrari dealership. I bought my car from him," Julian replied. "I got to know him and in the process, had the pleasure of meeting Mildred. We were just reminiscing about my car when you drove up."

"I'd give anything to see you whizzing up Main Street in it with your monk's robes on, Julian," said Mildred, "I really would. Anyway, it's so good to see you again. I still cannot get over the way you look, but, if there is one thing I have come to believe in after having been around schoolchildren for almost thirty years, it is the power we all have to work miracles in our lives. I'll leave you two gentlemen to yourselves. Drop by the dealership later, Julian. I'm sure Jack would be thrilled to see you," she said as she walked up the clean white stairs that led into the head office.

"I just might do that," Julian replied with a smile. "Now where were we, Peter? Oh yes. Ritual 7 in Yogi Raman's timeless leadership system. The seventh practice that visionary leaders have integrated into their routines to ensure that they perform as they should."

"You forgot to give me the next piece of the puzzle when you left me at Mount Percival. You've really kept me in suspense. All week, I've been coming up with different ideas about what Ritual 7 would be."

"Actually I didn't forget, Peter. I was hoping you would do precisely what you did since the seventh ritual is all about the power of ideas. Like I told you earlier, in the information era we currently find ourselves in, ideas rather than materials have become the commodity of success. For the first time in the history of our civilization, the real value of any company enters the building every morning and leaves the building every night. The highest assets of any organization lie within the skulls of its people."

"That's a graphic way of putting it. I don't think I'll forget that one for a while," I said with a smile.

"Good. I hope you don't because one of your most important tasks as a visionary leader is to unlock the natural state of creativity that sleeps within the minds of every one of your people. You must help your employees to think smarter and inspire them to explore new pathways of thought. Only then will you begin to experience the kind of innovation that you need to see before GlobalView grows into a world-class corporation."

"But is it really true that we are all creative? I mean, are you saying that every single one of my employees is capable of creative thinking? What about the accountants in our Finance Department or the lawyers on our legal staff? Surely they aren't creative types."

"You bet they are. It's just that they have probably never been encouraged to create and so their creativity has remained dormant. I myself used to think that only poets, writers, artists, and actors were the creative sort. Yogi Raman and the rest of the sages set me straight. They were the most creative people I've ever seen. The things they could come up with were amazing. Though they lived in an isolated part of the world, far removed from modern influences, they had fashioned brilliant tools and machinery to help them in their activities. While they lived very simple lives, they had crafted highly effective equipment to record their wisdom, to maintain high levels of hygiene, and to study the movements of the stars."

"Here we go with the stars again. When do you plan to tell me why you are so intrigued by the stars, in particular that bright one that pops up from time to time? My curiosity is starting to get the better of me, Julian," I pleaded.

"Next time for sure. For now, simply understand that every human being is endowed with creative tendencies. Begin to see your workplace as one giant idea factory, as a place where creativity and innovation are recognized and rewarded. Let your people know that they will now be allowed to take some risks. Teach them that failure is nothing more than learning how to win and that though some of the risks that they take may lead to setbacks, many will also lead to innovation. Spread this sentiment throughout the organization. Encourage creativity and make it clear that you are now open to listening to, understanding and implementing the best ideas of your people."

"Interesting. So risk taking is essential to innovation."

"Definitely. You can't get to third base with one foot on second. To remain competitive amid the idea era that modern business finds itself in, you and your managers must get your people to stretch themselves. You must give them the confidence they need to move out of their regions of security into uncharted places. You have to inspire them to be like butterflies, not barnacles."

"What do you mean?"

"Butterflies spend their days exploring new vistas and rising to new heights. Barnacles, on the other hand, attach themselves to one spot and remain there for the rest of their lives. By encouraging your people to take risks and by not punishing them if they encounter the failures that are inevitable, you will free them to explore their imaginations. Remember what Southwest did to that manager who came up with an innovative new program that unexpectedly failed?"

"They promoted him, right?"

"You got it. Don't tell me that doesn't inspire high levels of creativity and risk taking within the organization."

"Yes, it would. So the essence of creativity lies in taking risks?"

"That's just a part of what allows people to liberate the natural creativity that exists within them. The essence of creativity is really about originality of thought. Here," said Julian, reaching into his robe and pulling out the seventh piece of the puzzle. "Yogi Raman phrased the principle far more elegantly than I ever could."

The inscription on the puzzle was hard to make out. As I studied the wooden piece more closely, I was able to read what it said — *Ritual 7: See What All See, Think What None Think.*

"Just look at all these beautiful little children. They are all models of creativity, every single one of them. No one has rained on their parades and told them that the moon is not made of cheese or that Santa Claus does not exist. No one has stifled their dreams by telling them they cannot be doctors and lawyers or astronauts and movie actors. To them, the world contains boundless opportunities and endless possibilities. Their hearts are clean and their minds are pure. Study them carefully. Watch how they flex their imaginations. See how they give every ounce of their attention to what they do. Children come to us more highly evolved than adults to teach us the lessons we need to learn."

"I'd certainly agree with that, Julian. I remember when my kids were toddlers. I learned a lot from them back then."

"Like what?"

"I learned the importance of being curious, spontaneous, and playful. I guess I just never put it into practice. I also learned that there are always many ways of looking at something."

"Right. Yogi Raman shared a story with me one night that I'd like to pass on to you. A yogi was sitting with his disciples, high in the foothills of the Himalayas. As a test, he drew a line in the dirt and asked each student to make the line shorter without erasing any part of it. The students were perplexed and couldn't think of a way to shorten the line without touching it — except for one student. He had been the one who had studied the hardest and practiced the longest. He walked over to the line that the master had drawn and quickly drew a longer line next to it. He did not touch the first line in any way. The teacher smiled. 'Very good,' he said. 'Now the first line is shorter.'

"This kind of original thinking is what Ritual 7 is all about. See What All See, Think What None Think, the ritual of creativity and innovation, calls for you to begin to shed the shackles of the traditional ways of looking at things so that you can master the uncertainty that a changing business world brings. It's nothing more than developing the skill of discovering new solutions to old problems and finding smarter ways of doing what you do. It's about seeing things not as they are but as they can be. It's all about having the leadership courage to let a sense of childlike wonder fill the hearts and minds of your people.

"To foster innovation within GlobalView, *you must recognize that one of your highest priorities is to create a workplace that rewards curiosity and recognizes that new ideas are the seeds of success. Remember, even one good idea can totally transform your organization.* One brilliant new way to increase productivity or enhance quality can make a world of difference in your bottom line. Perhaps even more importantly, a truly original thought, properly executed, can change the lives of the many people your company has the privilege to serve. That's the real power of innovation. To make the world a better place. As Maya Angelou wrote so beautifully, 'If one is lucky, a solitary fantasy can totally transform one million realities.' "

"So where do I start?"

"First you must come to see every one of the people you lead as an artist."

"Really? Even the guys in sales and the folks in shipping?"

"Yes. As I have said earlier, awareness precedes change and if you do not grow intimately aware of the fact that every man and woman within the organization has the capacity to use his or her imagination to generate new ideas, GlobalView will never change into an innovation-centered company. Have the leadership wisdom to understand that all human beings are artists, capable of phenomenal levels of creativity when encouraged to think original thoughts. We all have the capacity for quantum levels of creativity.

"Just look at these kids," Julian said, pointing to the children scurrying around the playground, deeply absorbed in the games they were playing. "That little guy over there, strumming his imaginary guitar thinks he's the rock star he saw on the music video channel last night. That young girl by the tree believes she's a super hero, charged with saving the world from disaster. You can't tell me that each and every one of them is not an artist, a creator, rich with the ability to generate a fountain of delightful ideas at any given moment."

"True, but they're a bunch of children," I protested. "The people I lead are adults, the vast majority of whom appear to be incapable of thinking or doing anything out of the ordinary. Suggest that they try something new and they grow sweaty-palmed and frightened. They cling to their traditional ways of doing things as if their very lives depended on it, even if the new approach is a thousand times better."

"Whose fault is that?" Julian asked in a serious tone. *"Remember, the way you lead teaches your people how they must follow.* If that's how they react when you suggest that they stretch themselves a little, you and your managers have obviously not created an environment that is safe enough for them to explore new concepts with confidence. Perhaps they fear they will be punished should they fail. Perhaps their rigidity stems from the feeling that they will be ridiculed if they perform in a less than acceptable fashion. If your people are unwilling to embrace new ideas, concepts and systems with enthusiasm and energy, it's because you haven't taken the time to create a workplace that is risk-free. *Creativity is always stifled when people feel that they have something to lose.*"

"So how do I create a 'risk-free' environment?"

"There are many ways. Give your people the freedom to fail. Raise the level of trust. Celebrate spontaneity and reward original thinking. And let people be themselves. Give them permission to let the gifts of their imaginations shine."

"In an article I read a while ago, I remember the CEO of Reebok, Paul Fireman, saying that the secret to the company's success was that the employees were given the freedom to create. 'Ordinary people went way beyond themselves only because they were allowed to do it,' he reflected."

"Precisely. Remember, visionary leaders never manage creativity — they simply uncover it and allow it to flood the organization. They unleash it, in the hope that their companies will become dynamic playgrounds of innovation, much like the one we are now standing in."

Just as Julian completed his sentence, a spoonful of thick pudding whizzed through the air and landed on the sleeve of his immaculate red robe. The culprit, a small boy with a devilish grin, let out a loud cheer the moment he realized he had connected with his intended target. He then turned around and ran as fast as his little legs would carry him, all the while yelling, "I got the monk! I got the monk! I got the monk!"

Julian just stood there, startled. Then, true to form, he reached over and dipped a finger into the slippery mess running down his robe. "Hope it's chocolate," he said with a laugh. "It always was my favorite flavor.

"That actually leads me to another key point about fostering creativity within your workplace, Peter," continued Julian, mopping up the remains of the pudding with a crisp white hankie I had pulled out of the suit jacket I was wearing. "In order for your company to become the 'playground of ideas' that will skyrocket it to world-class status, the environment you provide for your people to work in must be a fun one. You see, one of the great barriers to creativity is the belief that playfulness is reserved for kids. That kind of thinking not only limits creativity, it increases workplace stress. There's nothing wrong with people letting their hair down from time to time and enjoying a solid belly laugh. There's nothing wrong with letting people have fun at work. *Work should be fun.* And allowing people the chance to have fun through their work is a brilliant leadership philosophy because it will confirm to all that you truly do put people first. It shows you care. Hugo Rahner said: 'To play is to yield oneself to a kind of magic' and Plato observed that 'life should be lived as play.' Remember, the men and women you lead spend the majority of their lives at the office. The least you can do is make it a great place to be. Fun and laughter are door-ways to the hearts and imaginations of your people. *And people love doing business with people who love their business."*

"Great point, Julian. What other tips do you have to help me unleash the creativity and energy of our people?"

"Here's a few quick thoughts that will help you revitalize and reenergize your workplace. Encourage your people to set a weekly 'idea quota' for themselves. Develop a formalized system to reward the best ideas so that people learn their originality matters. Organize monthly outings for the people in your different divisions to keep things interesting and build team unity. Visit a comedy club or rent a movie theater or have a beach party — at the office. I also recommend you set up a contest committee. That's when the good times really start."

"A contest committee?"

"Yes, a committee that dreams up all sorts of fun and playful contests that will make your people laugh and smile and grow to love working at your company. It's a great way to increase job satisfaction and reduce turnover. It will even help you win more customers."

"Really?"

"Sure. *Never forget that when you ensure that your employees laugh while they work, they will ensure that your clients laugh while they buy.* Are you beginning to see how a positive work environment not only boosts creativity and innovation but also the bottom line?"

"I am."

"Just think about how great Ugliest Tie Day or Funniest Joke Week or Free Pancake Morning, where everyone would be treated to pancakes prepared by you and your management team, would be for the hearts and spirits of your people? Imagine letting the people in production have half an hour off late one Friday afternoon to have a paper-airplane flying contest if they meet a specified quota. I'd be willing to bet that they'd not only meet but exceed it. And if you really want to telegraph the fact that your attitude has improved and you want people to have more fun, you might even do a '4-4-5-4-9-8.' "

"What's a 4-4-5-4-9-8?"

"It's the tune to Happy Birthday on the keypad of your telephone. Imagine playing it for one of your employees on her birthday as you wish her well. It would be unbelievable wouldn't it?"

"*Unbelievable* is what my people would think."

"Remember, if your people rediscover the playfulness they knew as kids while they are at work, they will be much happier. Happier employees are more creative, productive and loyal. And creative, productive and loyal people are at the foundation of every truly great organization. Right?"

"Right."

"Just remember that *the company that plays together stays together.*"

"Oh, and from time to time," added Julian as he walked me back to my car while the school kids waved, "treat yourself to some great questions."

"What do you mean?"

"Creative questioning is one of the finest methods to keep your thinking fresh and original. Smart questions help to get you out of your regions of security into the zone of the unknown, that place where your perspective shifts and all things are possible."

"Can you suggest a few questions for me to consider?"

"Sure. How about, 'What would I do if I knew I could not fail?' Or consider, 'What three things could I do every week, which, if I really did well, would change my leadership effectiveness?' Then ask yourself why you are not doing them. When you face a problem, why not ask yourself, 'How might Kennedy, Churchill or

Confucius have handled this?' And perhaps the best question to ask yourself when it comes to challenging yourself to rise to higher levels of creative achievement is: *'What would the child that I once was think of the adult that I have become?'* "

"That's quite a question, Julian," I said softly as we reached my car, "I'm almost ashamed to answer it."

"Nourish your imagination and flex your mind. Let your natural curiosity out of the box again. Dare to dream bigger dreams and envision a higher future. Although you might see what every other leader in the business world sees, start to think what no one else is thinking. Never forget that deep within the body of every truly visionary leader lives the spirit of a little child, full of excitement and wonder. The sense of energy, optimism, and hope you will generate will be contagious. You owe it to the men and women who look to you for leadership."

"You really seem to believe that a leader who has 'hope' can make a world of difference, don't you?"

"Absolutely. Hope is a fuel that drives visionary leaders and vision-led companies. It reminds me of what one old man said near the end of his life, 'I am an average person with below-average capabilities. I have not the shadow of a doubt that any man or woman can achieve what I have if he or she would put forth the same effort and cultivate the same hope and faith.' "

"Was that one of those rich business executives you used to represent in your former glory days?"

"No, Peter," Julian replied, pausing for a moment. "Those were the words of Gandhi."

"Remarkable," I replied quietly. "Speaking of hope, I remember glancing at the paper recently and seeing a headline that read, 'Paralyzed Journalist Wrote Book by Blinking.' "

"Really?"

"Yes. It was the story of Jean-Dominique Bauby, the former chief editor at *Elle* magazine in Paris. While driving his son into the city one morning, he suffered a massive stroke and collapsed in the back seat of his car while his frightened son ran to get help. Three weeks later, he emerged from a coma speechless, nearly deaf and paralyzed. He couldn't move any part of his body — except for one."

"Which was?" asked Julian, hanging on my every word.

"His left eyelid. And given his abundance of hope and optimism along with his deep desire to make a difference, Jean-Dominique decided that though he could not move, he would somehow find a way to write a book so that he could share the wisdom he had discovered from his tragedy with others. Using the power of his creative imagination to think of ways to fulfill his dream, he eventually stumbled upon the solution: he would create a special alphabet where each letter would correspond to certain blinks of his eyelid."

"You're kidding?"

"No, it's absolutely true," I replied. "For three hours every single day with an editor by his side in a dark hospital room, this man slowly blinked his way through his book. The newspaper estimated that Jean-Dominique blinked more than 200,000 times to produce his 137-page text. And by all accounts, the work is a masterpiece.

"In it he wrote about all the things he had always wanted to do in his life but had never done: climbing an Alpine peak with the Tour de France cyclists, racing down a Formula One speedway, or enjoying a Lyonnais sausage on a beautiful summer's day. And he expressed his pain at not being able to hold his young children anymore and play their games and be the kind of person he had wanted to be."

"After completion of the book," I continued, "he founded an association to help other paralyzed victims and their families, dedicating himself to transforming his adversity into a victory by inspiring others through the power of his example. Sadly, Jean-Dominique passed away — the article I read was actually his obituary. But I know you'll agree, Julian, that his life stands as a shining tribute to the strength of the human spirit to achieve the kinds of things you have been teaching me about. His act of personal heroism really is what See What All See, Think What None Think is all about, isn't it?"

"Yes, Peter, that's exactly what Ritual 7 is about. Finding great opportunity where others see only tragic adversity. Finding hope where others feel only despair. Seeing light where others see only darkness. That's a moving example. I thank you for sharing it with me. You know, what people can accomplish while fueled by a compelling and worthy cause never ceases to amaze me. What does surprise me, though, is that most people wait until they face some kind of a crisis, whether professional or personal, before they reach deep within themselves and discover their human gifts. It's really quite sad."

As I sat in the driver's seat of my car and rolled down the window, Julian stooped over, placing his hands on his knees.

"Well, my friend, we have only one meeting left before I have to head on to my next destination. It has been a true joy spending time with you. I'm glad to see my leadership wisdom is having such a positive impact on GlobalView."

"I'll never be able to thank you enough, Julian," I replied gratefully.

"Just keep putting the lessons I've been sharing into practice and sharing the philosophy of the sages with all those around you.

Let the leadership truths they discovered spread throughout your organization and into the business community. Tell as many leaders and managers as you can about this timeless knowledge. That will be thanks enough."

"Aren't you forgetting something?" I asked as Julian began to walk away.

"I know, I know. You want to know where to meet me next, right?"

"You got it. I'm not missing the last ritual for the world."

"Our final meeting will take place out at the observatory. Meet me there at midnight. I'll show you something that will change the way you think about leadership forever."

"Really?"

"Really. Oh, and before you go, you better take this little piece of wood I've been carrying around. I know how much you like making jigsaw puzzles," he said with a wink.

Julian reached into his robe, pulled out the final piece of the jigsaw puzzle and pressed it gently into my left hand. "Until next time, amigo."

I looked down at the simple gift my friend had bestowed on me. These pieces had come to have great meaning for me and served as powerful reminders of the rituals of visionary leaders that I had learned to date. The eighth one contained a faint design that, as with each of the others, I had difficulty making out. It also carried a message as mysterious as the previous seven. It read simply, *Ritual 8: Link Leadership to Legacy.*

I quickly looked up to ask him what these words meant, but he had vanished. The only soul that remained in the playground was now standing silently in front of me. It was a gentle little boy. He just looked at me and smiled.

Chapter 11 Knowledge Summary • Julian's Wisdom in a Nutshell

The Ritual

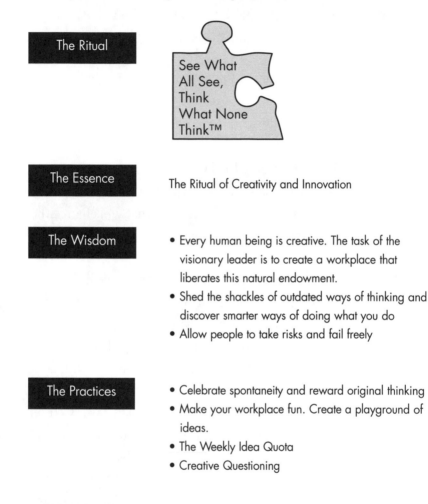

See What
All See,
Think
What None
Think™

The Essence

The Ritual of Creativity and Innovation

The Wisdom

- Every human being is creative. The task of the visionary leader is to create a workplace that liberates this natural endowment.
- Shed the shackles of outdated ways of thinking and discover smarter ways of doing what you do
- Allow people to take risks and fail freely

The Practices

- Celebrate spontaneity and reward original thinking
- Make your workplace fun. Create a playground of ideas.
- The Weekly Idea Quota
- Creative Questioning

Quotable Quote

Nourish your imagination and flex your mind. Let your natural creativity out of the box. Dare to dream bigger dreams and envision a higher future. Though you might see what every other leader in the business world sees, start to think what no one else thinks. Never forget that deep within the body of every visionary leader lives the spirit of a little child, full of excitement and wonder.

The Monk Who Sold His Ferrari

RITUAL 8

༄

Link Leadership to Legacy

CHAPTER TWELVE

The Ritual of Contribution and Significance

I cannot believe that the purpose of life is to be "Happy." I think the purpose of life is to be useful, to be responsible, to be compassionate. It is, above all, to matter: to count, to stand for something, to have made some difference that you have lived at all.

Leo C. Rosten

IT WAS JUST BEFORE MIDNIGHT when I drove up the long winding road that led to the observatory. Located out in the country, it usually sat empty except for the two astronomers who used it as their research base. I quickly parked my car and rushed up the stairs that would lead me into the main hall where Julian had instructed me to meet him promptly. The night was a spectacular one, with not a cloud in the sky. Even to the naked eye, the heavens were alight with the moon and the stars. I knew Julian would be pleased.

"Hi, Peter," Julian mumbled as he offered me a quick welcome before returning his concentration to the sights he had been observing through the massive telescope. "Glad that you could make it."

"I wouldn't have missed it for anything, my friend. Is there something in particular that we are looking for tonight?"

"Oh, yes. Tonight will be a very special evening. That I can promise you," he replied, not taking his eyes away from the telescope.

"You'll be happy to hear that, with the last piece of the puzzle you gave me, I finally got the whole thing together."

"And what did you discover?"

"Well, every time you gave me a new piece with one of the eight rituals carved into it, I could also detect some form of design on it. But I was never able to quite figure out what it was. As the pieces came together, I could see it was turning into a symbol of some sort, but without the last piece, I still couldn't tell what it was."

"And now do you know?"

"It's a star."

"Not just a star, my friend. It's *the* star."

"I'm not sure that I follow you, Julian."

"Every star in the moonlit sky is bright. But one star in particular is brilliant."

"Which one's that?"

"It is the North Star, the most luminescent of them all."

Suddenly Julian let out a yell. "There it is! It's time! Let's go," he cried, leading me by the arm as he ran out of the building. We raced down the steps and along a winding path that led us into a vast field. Then we stopped and just stood there in silence.

"It's happening just like the sages promised it would," remarked Julian with delight.

"What's happening?" I asked, not observing anything out of the ordinary.

"This," he said, as he pointed up to a star that was beginning to flicker against the rich black coat of darkness that had dominated the evening sky. Growing brighter and brighter, its light started to flood the dark summer sky. Soon the star became so bright that I had to raise my hand in an effort to shield my eyes. It was a little like what had happened the night of the basketball game but a hundred times more intense. Before long, the entire sky was filled with light and it appeared as if it was the middle of the day, even though the dial on my watch indicated that it was a quarter past midnight. It was an unbelievable sight.

Looking over at Julian, I saw that he was beaming, his face full of joy and excitement. A radiant smile appeared on his youthful face and his hands were clasped together in the traditional way that the citizens of India greeted those they respected.

"Savor what you are seeing, Peter. The world won't see anything like this for another thousand years. The sages, in their infinite wisdom, had known this astronomical event would take place on this very night at this very time. I'm sure they must be experiencing it now, high up in their part of the world, just as we are witnessing it now in ours. I hope they're as moved by it as I am. I sure do miss them."

"What's this all about?" I asked, quickly looking back up at the sky before I lost another second.

"This, my friend, is nature's way of bringing in the dawn of a new era, a new age of leadership and life. There has been so much turmoil and turbulence in the world that many good people are giving up hope. They are losing faith in their power to make a difference. They are giving in to the demands of uncertainty and negativity, rather than transcending them and moving on to higher places of achievement, contribution and success. Many people in our society are even giving up on the gift of living. The natural phenomenon we're witnessing will act as a torchlight to remind leaders of their obligation to be visionaries. It will serve as their wake-up call to be the forces of good they are meant to be, illuminating their organizations just as the North Star has illuminated the sky on this very special night. Be a light, Peter. Be the one people look up to for guidance and direction. Let the ideal you aspire to burn brightly within you, blazing a path for all to see. This is your ultimate purpose in leadership — and in life."

Just as Julian had delivered this profound piece of wisdom, the night returned to its normal condition. We sat on the grass, Julian's robe growing creased and wrinkled. Then he continued, "One of the most timeless of all of the leadership laws is this one: *The Purpose of Life Is a Life of Purpose.*"

"Powerful statement."

"The greatest irony of leadership is that the more you give, the more you get. And when all is said and done, the highest and most enduring gift that you will ever be able to give is the gift of what you leave behind. Your legacy to the generations that follow will be how much value you have added to your organization and how many lives you have improved. As the great humanitarian Albert Schweitzer observed: 'There is no higher religion than human service. To work for the common good is the greatest creed.' Or perhaps even more to the point, let me use the words one father offered to his son while he lay on his deathbed: 'Be ashamed to die until you have scored a victory for mankind.' "

"So you're saying that visionary leaders, in practicing Ritual 8, link what they do with who they will serve."

"Nicely put, Peter. And in constantly focusing on leaving a rich footprint of service and contribution behind them when they depart, *such leaders link leadership to legacy*. In doing so, they fulfill their calling. They fulfill their duty to liberate the fullness of their personal gifts for a worthy cause. All the great leaders who have gone before us have aspired to reach this pinnacle, whether they were leaders in business, the sciences or even the arts. Just before his death, George Bernard Shaw was asked what he would do if he could live his life again. Though he had already achieved more in his lifetime than most of us could only dream of, he replied humbly, 'I would want to be the person I could have been but was not.' "

"Wise words," I replied.

"They are. They make me think of a short story penned by Leo Tolstoy called 'The Death of Ivan Ilych.' Ever read it?"

"No, Julian. To be honest I've never read any of Tolstoy's works. I guess I've never got around to it."

"There's such wisdom in the great books of literature and yet most people seem to be too busy to discover it. And so they continue to make mistakes both in their leadership and in their lives, mistakes that could so easily have been prevented had they taken a few hours out of their weeks to read deeply. In this particular story, Tolstoy wrote about Ivan Ilych, a vain, highly materialistic social climber who was more concerned about appearing successful than doing right. As a young man, he married, not because he loved and cherished his wife, but because high society approved of the match. He then had a number of kids, not because he wanted to have children but because that was what was expected of him. Rather than spending time with his family and building a rich home life, he devoted almost all his time to his work, becoming obsessed with his public persona as a top-level government lawyer.

Robin Sharma

"Soon, in an effort to keep up appearances, he began to live beyond his means, and eventually faced enormous financial hardship. This led to deep unhappiness and despair. As luck would have it, just when things were at their worst, he was offered a more prestigious and much higher-paying position as a judge. With his newfound good fortune, he bought the house of his dreams. He felt very proud of it and began to devote much of his time to furnishing the home with expensive antiques and fashionable furniture. The house had to be perfect, so all those around him would be suitably impressed.

"One day, when he was climbing a stepladder to show an upholsterer how he wanted a set of draperies hung, he fell and hurt his side. After the fall, he felt different and grew ill-tempered, often lashing out at his wife for the smallest transgression. A visit to a doctor revealed that he was seriously ill and various treatments were prescribed. But Ivan Ilych's condition only worsened. Within months, the once vital and jovial man appeared to be dying, his eyes lacking any expression of life and his body growing terribly weak. In his quiet agony, Ivan Ilych began to reflect on his life. First he thought about his childhood, then about his days as a striving adult and finally he contemplated the sad state he found himself in. Suddenly a question flooded his consciousness. A question that penetrated the deepest core of his being."

"What was it?"

"He asked himself this: *'What if my whole life has really been wrong?'* You see, Peter, for the first time in his life, he realized that all his jockeying for social position, all the energy he spent trying to look good and to be seen with the right people at the right events, was really not important. This dying man realized that life is a gift. And his could have been so much more than he had made of it. He could have contributed immensely and served greatly. He could have risked, dared, and dreamed. He could have been the person he should have been. Instead, he squandered his days on frivolous matters of little consequence, matters that did nothing to improve the world around him. With that realization, his physical pain grew even worse and his mental torment became unbearable. He began to scream, and continued to do so for three full days.

"Then just two hours before his death," continued Julian, "he said to himself, 'Yes, it was all not the right thing.' He then grew silent and wondered, 'But what *is* the right thing?' Just then his young son, a schoolboy who had been deeply saddened by his father's illness, crept softly into the room and stood beside his bed. His father put a frail hand on the boy's head as the child began to cry. At that moment, a timeless truth was revealed to Ivan Ilych, one that most people never discover. He realized that although he had not lived his life as he should have lived, *it was still not too late to rectify his failure.* He realized that his duty was to serve all those around him and to enrich their lives in any way possible. He understood that the purpose of life was to make a difference through one's presence. If even one life was left a little better, it would have been worth living. So as his final act, he requested that his son leave the room so he would not have to endure any more of his father's suffering. He then closed his eyes and died."

I was deeply moved by this story. The power of the message Julian had just shared was not lost on me. I looked up at the sky, breathing in the fresh air and staring at nature's abundance. I reflected on all the time that had passed in my life and on all the things I had missed. I thought about the many men and women who counted on me and considered the duty I owed to them. I thought about the enormous potential of our company and regretted all the opportunities we had neglected. My thoughts then turned to my family. A lump came to my throat when I considered all of those special times I had missed with my two young sons. Little-league baseball games, Christmas concerts, sun-filled afternoons laughing in the park were all missed because I had not had the courage to spend my life well. I thought of my youngest son whose only request of me was to play and laugh a little more with him. I thought about his elder brother whom I had not spent even one quiet evening with in many months. I thought about Samantha and all the romantic getaways that I had promised we would go on, but never did. I really had missed out on living the life I was meant to live.

But, as Ivan Ilych came to appreciate, it was never too late to do what is right and live life fully. That moment I vowed to change the very person I was. I would become the kind of leader my heart told me I was capable of being. I promised myself I would be the kind of husband and father I knew I had the capacity to become. And I would live with the kind of soaring intensity I knew I deserved. At that moment, I looked over at Julian. Tears filled his eyes as well.

"I think you now understand what I've been saying, my friend. To be the kind of person that you are destined to be and to leave something special behind for all those who follow you is what life's all about. It is the essence of leaving a legacy. As Yogi Raman put it, *'What makes greatness is beginning something that does not end with you.'* "

"You know, Julian," I said as I wiped my eyes, "my dad used to say that 'the first fifty years of life are spent building one's legitimacy while the last fifty are to be devoted to building one's legacy.' I never quite understood what he meant until now."

"The sages had a saying that captures the essence of the point that your father in all his wisdom was trying to make."

"What was it?"

"They used to tell me that 'when you were born, the world rejoiced while you cried. Your mission must be to live your life in such a way that when you die, the world cries while you rejoice.' Only then will your life have made the difference it was intended to make."

"Just so I am perfectly clear, Julian, will my legacy then be the goals that I will have achieved over my life as a leader?"

"Your legacy must be so much more than that. Your legacy will ultimately be a manifestation of the deepest and the best that you had to give in life. It will be a reflection of the person you now are and the person you aim to be. Leaving a legacy is not about impressing your friends or reaching the top. It's not about looking good but about doing good. It's more about fulfilling your duty and actualizing your humanity. Legacy-Based Leadership is the most powerful type of leadership. Practicing it will allow you to do what few leaders in the world today can do."

"Which is?"

"*To create a successful present while building a brilliant future.* And if I may say so, Peter, every leader in every field of endeavor should aspire to no less."

Julian then walked me back to the entrance of the observatory. Under the steps was a little wooden box that had been covered by a clean white cloth. Julian reached down and picked the box up, carefully making sure that the precious contents were given their due respect.

"Here, this is for you. The time has finally come for me to leave and for you to explore the full magnificence of the 8 Rituals of Visionary Leaders on your own. I could not have asked for a better student and a more receptive friend. From the day I first exposed you to the leadership wisdom of the sages at our golf club, to this evening here at the observatory, you have embraced what I have come to share with an open mind and an honest heart.

"And so, as a token of my thanks for allowing me to fulfill my promise to Yogi Raman and spread the lessons I learned throughout our part of the world, I humbly offer you this gift. It has great meaning to me and has been my constant companion since I left the Himalayas. I couldn't think of a better home for it than with you. All I ask is that you sincerely continue to apply the knowledge that I have delivered to you and spread The 8 Rituals of Visionary Leaders throughout your organization for all to discover. In this way, not only will you transform your leadership, you will bless the lives of all those around you."

And with those final words, Julian reached over and embraced me as only a dear friend could, then dashed off into the darkness, his richly embroidered robe trailing behind him. As I opened the box, I saw that the gift was beautifully wrapped in some type of homemade covering. I immediately removed it, eager to find the special present Julian had placed within.

As I looked deeper, I saw that the box held a shiny object. A smile came to my face as I recognized what it was. It was the small telescope that Julian had been clinging to the night of the basketball game. I could not believe that he would have parted with such a prized possession. I knew how much his stargazing had meant to him.

Picking it up, I noticed that an inscription had been engraved on the telescope in elegant lettering. It said simply: *To my now wise friend, Peter, a man who I know will touch many lives. May your spark of leadership turn fear into power and darkness into light. With love, your fan, Julian.*

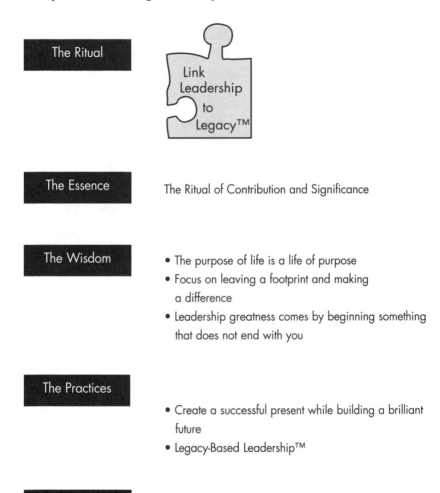

| The Ritual | Link Leadership to Legacy™ |

The Essence

The Ritual of Contribution and Significance

The Wisdom

- The purpose of life is a life of purpose
- Focus on leaving a footprint and making a difference
- Leadership greatness comes by beginning something that does not end with you

The Practices

- Create a successful present while building a brilliant future
- Legacy-Based Leadership™

Quotable Quote

Your legacy will ultimately be a manifestation of the deepest and the best that you had to give in life. It will be a reflection of the person you now are and the person you aim to be. Leaving a legacy is not about impressing your friends or reaching the top. It's not about looking good but about doing good. It's about fulfilling your duty and actualizing your humanity.

The Monk Who Sold His Ferrari

THE 8 RITUALS OF VISIONARY LEADERS™

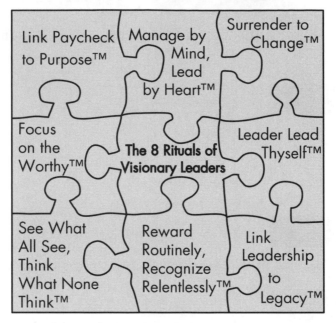

1. Link Paycheck to Purpose™
   (The Ritual of a Compelling Future Focus)

2. Manage by Mind, Lead by Heart™
   (The Ritual of Human Relations)

3. Reward Routinely, Recognize Relentlessly™
   (The Ritual of Team Unity)

4. Surrender to Change™
   (The Ritual of Adaptability and Change Management)

5. Focus on the Worthy™
   (The Ritual of Personal Effectiveness)

6. Leader Lead Thyself™
   (The Ritual of Self-Leadership)

7. See What All See, Think What None Think™
   (The Ritual of Creativity and Innovation)

8. Link Leadership to Legacy™
   (The Ritual of Contribution and Significance)

THE SHARMA LEADERSHIP REPORT™

FREE subscription offer to purchasers of *Leadership Wisdom from The Monk Who Sold His Ferrari* for a limited time only. (Annual subscription has a $95 value.)

The Sharma Leadership Report, Robin Sharma's hugely popular electronic newsletter, is packed with practical wisdom, lessons, and tips that you can apply immediately to improve the quality of your life. This highly inspirational report focuses on leading-edge topics for personal, professional, and character develop-ment including self-esteem, inner renewal, peak performance, discipline, creativity, life-career balance, relationships, self-leadership, stress mastery, and career leadership. Join the thousands who love this extra-ordinary learning tool!

To order your free subscription, simply visit **www.robinsharma.com** and register on-line today.

KEYNOTES & SEMINARS WITH ROBIN SHARMA

#1 Bestselling Author & Professional Speaker

Robin Sharma is one of North America's most thought-provoking and electrifying professional speakers. His powerful wisdom and pioneering insights on leadership, managing rapid change, personal effectiveness, and life renewal have made him the first choice of organizations seeking a high-profile keynote speaker or seminar leader whose message will transform lives and restore commitment in these turbulent times. Robin Sharma's enormously inspirational presentations are fully customized through a unique research process, rich in practical content and designed to help your people rise to all-new levels of perfromance, passion, creativity, and personal fulfillment.

To book Robin for your next conference or in-house seminar, visit **www.robinsharma.com** or call:

Marnie Ballane
V.P. of Speaking Services
Sharma Leadership International
Telephone: 1-888-RSHARMA (774-2762)
E-mail: marnie@robinsharma.com

PERSONAL COACHING
WITH ROBIN SHARMA

1. THE MONTHLY COACH™

The Monthly Coach is Robin's highly acclaimed book- and CD-of-the-month club. Each month, you receive one of the most powerful books available on personal development and self-discovery, along with a CD recording of Robin's summary of the book's best points and his insights on how to translate the book's knowledge into real results in your life. This program is life changing.

2. THE ROBIN SHARMA LIFE COACHING PROCESS™

This is Robin's revolutionary system for people who are ready to create extraordinary lives. You meet with Robin in a small group setting every three months over the course of a year to experience one of the most effective programs for personal transformation and self-renewal available today. Also available in a three-day format.

3. THE ELITE PERFORMERS SERIES™

The Elite Performers Series is Sharma Leadership International's flagship corporate coaching program, which is designed to transform employees into leaders who excel amid change. Presented by Robin to your organization's employees, over four incredible days The Elite Performers Series will inspire your team to operate at all-new levels of effectiveness, excellence, and personal responsibility. This is one of the best leadership training programs available today.

4. THE MASTERS SERIES

This is an exclusive program for executives and entrepreneurs seeking world-class, one-on-one coaching to create extraordinary results both professionally and personally. You meet weekly with one of our Lead Coaches via telephone or the Internet and experience a powerful process that has helped thousands of people transform the way they think, feel, and act. Robin Sharma himself accepts up to five executive coaching clients each year to serve as their personal life coach. The results are always the same: complete life transformation.

For more information on these personal coaching options, please contact our Vice-President of Coaching Services, Al Moscardelli, at:

Sharma Leadership International
Toll-free: 1-888-RSHARMA (774-2762)
e-mail: coaching@robinsharma.com
Website: **www.robinsharma.com**

POWERFUL WISDOM FOR LEADERSHIP
IN BUSINESS AND IN LIFE

NOW AVAILABLE IN ALL GOOD BOOKSTORES

Discounts available on quantity purchases for your
organization. Please call 1-888-RSHARMA
or e-mail info@robinsharma.com for pricing information.

WE HAVE A REQUEST

Robin Sharma would love to hear how this book has affected both you and your organization. Share your success stories, insights, and experiences. Do you have a tip or quotes that you would like to share with other readers in Robin's popular newsletter, *The Sharma Leadership Report*™? Please send them to us. Robin will make every possible effort to respond with a personal note. We want to hear from you!

Please connect with Robin by sending him an e-mail. His direct address is: **wisdom@robinsharma.com.** You can also mail him a letter c/o:

Sharma Leadership International
304 Newbury Street, #519
Boston, MA 02115-2832
Toll-free: 1-888-RSHARMA (774-2762)
Website: **www.robinsharma.com**

For Robin's latest thinking on personal leadership and life management, visit **www.robinsharma.com**, one of the Internet's most popular destinations for personal success and professional mastery.

ABOUT ROBIN SHARMA

Robin Sharma is one of the world's premier thinkers on leadership in business and in life. He is the author of numerous books, including the #1 international bestseller *The Monk Who Sold His Ferrari*; its bestselling sequel *Leadership Wisdom from The Monk Who Sold His Ferrari*; *Family Wisdom from The Monk Who Sold His Ferrari*; *Who Will Cry When You Die?*, *The Saint, the Surfer, and the CEO*; and *Begin Within*. Sharma is also in constant demand across the globe as a keynote speaker for organizations dedicated to developing leaders at all levels and as an executive coach to people ready to create extraordinary work and personal lives. Clients include Fortune 500 companies such as Microsoft, General Motors, IBM, FedEx, as well as leading trade associations.

A former lawyer who holds two law degrees, including a master's of law, Robin Sharma is the CEO of Sharma Leadership International (SLI), a widely respected training firm that offers a range of services and products to help employees realize their highest potential for exceptional professional and personal results amidst relentless change, including The Elite Performers Series™, a remarkable four-day leadership transformation program. SLI also runs the highly acclaimed *Robin Sharma Life Coaching Program*™, a strikingly effective coaching process that shows individuals and corporate teams how to create the personal lives they want while becoming a star at work. Sharma Leadership International also offers *The Monthly Coach* program—the acclaimed book/CD-of-the-month club where Robin personally selects a life changing work that will enhance your growth and enrich your life. He will send it to you every 30 days for continual improvement. For more information on any of these services or to see our complete line of learning products, please visit **www.robin-sharma.com** or call **1-888-RSHARMA**.

***

We hope you enjoyed this Hay House book.
If you would like to receive a free catalog
featuring additional Hay House books and
products, or if you would like information about
the Hay Foundation, please contact:

Hay House, Inc.
P.O. Box 5100
Carlsbad, CA 92018-5100

(760) 431-7695 or (800) 654-5126
(760) 431-6948 (fax) or (800) 650-5115 (fax)
www.hayhouse.com

***

Published and distributed in Australia by: Hay House Australia
Pty Ltd, P.O. Box 515, Brighton-Le-Sands, NSW 2216
phone: 1800 023 516 • *e-mail:* info@hayhouse.com.au

Distributed in the United Kingdom by: Airlift, 8 The Arena,
Mollison Ave., Enfield, Middlesex,
United Kingdom EN3 7NL

***